Memory and Autobiography

Critical South

The publication of this series is supported by the International Consortium of Critical Theory Programs funded by the Andrew W. Mellon Foundation.

Series editors:
Natalia Brizuela and Leticia Sabsay

Memory and Autobiography

Explorations at the Limits

Leonor Arfuch

Translated by Christina MacSweeney

polity

Originally published in Spanish as *Memoria y autobiografia: Exploraciones en los límites*
© Fondo de Cultura Económica de Argentina, 2013

This English edition © 2020 by Polity Press

The research that gave rise to this book was carried out with a grant from The John Simon Guggenheim Memorial Foundation in 2007

Polity Press
65 Bridge Street
Cambridge CB2 1UR, UK

Polity Press
101 Station Landing
Suite 300
Medford, MA 02155, USA

ISBN-13: 978-1-5095-4217-8 hardback
ISBN-13: 978-1-5095-4218-5 paperback

A catalogue record for this book is available from the British Library.

Library of Congress Cataloging-in-Publication Data

Names: Arfuch, Leonor, author. | MacSweeney, Christina, translator.
Title: Memory and autobiography : explorations in the limits / Leonor Arfuch ; translated by Christina MacSweeney.
Other titles: Memoria y autobiografía. English
Description: Cambridge ; Medford, MA : Polity, [2020] | Series: Critical south | "Originally published in Spanish as Memoria y autobiografia: Exploraciones en los límites © Fondo de Cultura Económica de Argentina, 2013" | Includes bibliographical references and index. | Summary: "A leading Argentinian scholar examines the role of biography and autobiography in contemporary culture"-- Provided by publisher.
Identifiers: LCCN 2020005859 (print) | LCCN 2020005860 (ebook) | ISBN 9781509542178 (hardback) | ISBN 9781509542185 (paperback) | ISBN 9781509542192 (epub)
Subjects: LCSH: Autobiography. | Biography as a literary form. | Biography   in art. | Memory (Philosophy)
Classification: LCC CT25 .A7413 2020 (print) | LCC CT25 (ebook) | DDC 808.06/692--dc23
LC record available at https://lccn.loc.gov/2020005859
LC ebook record available at https://lccn.loc.gov/2020005860

Typeset in 10.5 on 12pt Sabon LT Pro
by Fakenham Prepress Solutions, Fakenham, Norfolk NR21 8NL
Printed and bound in Great Britain by TJ International Limited

For further information on Polity, visit our website: politybooks.com

Contents

The world that came like a bird
has alighted on my shoulder
and I tremble like a branch
under the weight of the song
and the flight, detained for an instant.

Rosario Castellanos (1998)[1]

---

[1] El mundo que venía como un pájaro / se ha posado en mi hombro / y yo tiemblo lo mismo que una rama / bajo el peso del canto / y del vuelo un instante detenido.

Acknowledgements

I would particularly like to thank Adriana Rodríguez Périsco, Mariana Wikinski, Héctor Schmucler (in memoriam), Aída Loya, María Stegmayer and Micaela Cuesta for the close readings and suggestions that accompanied the journeys this book has taken.

Introduction

Leonor Arfuch is one of the founding intellectuals of post-dictatorship thought in Argentina. Her work, like that of any great theoretician or thinker, reads like a gradual unfolding and deepening of certain questions that seem to have been there from the very beginning – questions about politics, art, language, memory, the image, ethics and the self.

Having lived through the tumultuous years of military dictatorship in her country (1976–1983) – years in which the persecution of leftist militants, torture, forced disappearance, exile and the kidnapping of children were commonplace – Arfuch's critical passions emerged as a response to a present in crisis, as a means to think through that present and intervene in it so as to open greater spaces for the democratization of thought and political action. It therefore shouldn't be surprising that a beautifully edited book she published in 2005 bears the title *Pensar este tiempo: espacios, afectos, pertenencias* (*To Think This Time: Space, Affections, Belonging*).[1] Edited during an academic stay in 2004 as a fellow of the British Academy, the book brings together essays by prominent intellectuals of Great Britain and continental Europe (Scott Lash, Doreen Massey, William Rowe, Chantal Mouffe and others) in an exploration of the relationships among politics, emotions and aesthetics in a political present in which the social bond is under siege by conservative political forces and the power of capital. Arfuch's vision leaves no doubt about the far-reaching implications of her theoretical contributions and intellectual inquiry. The book's title is telling. To think about *this* time, *our* time – a time of crisis, inequality, globalization, capital, war, displacement of peoples, gender inequity, racism and xenophobia – drives her critical act and nourishes her writing to this day. In this sense, the problems she addresses are not just those of Argentina but those of Latin America and the world, always attentive to how *here* and *there*, *you* and *I*, connect with or diverge from one another.

Like many thinkers 'schooled' under dictatorship, Leonor Arfuch was, in a certain sense and by necessity, an autodidact. From the mid-1960s until the early 1970s, she expressed her political commitments by association with the left. Persecution, of course, was a frequent and constant threat in those years against anyone who openly identified with the left, and universities did not escape the repression. In an environment in which many university professors had been expelled from their posts or suffered direct reprisals by the military junta and its henchmen, Arfuch completed her undergraduate studies in literature at the University of Buenos Aires while the regime was still in power. Though her life in those years transpired with a certain degree of 'normalcy', a thoroughly violent atmosphere, coupled with her personal history of militancy, left her acutely aware of what was happening around her and inspired in her both a tenacious rebelliousness and a desire to critique that have marked her professional trajectory and writings. Under dictatorship, Arfuch worked with important mentors such as the famed Argentine critic Josefina Ludmer (1939–2016), whose 'underground' study groups became lovingly known in Argentina as the 'university of the catacombs' (*la universidad de las catacumbas*). In such spaces, many of the country's foremost intellectuals, like Arfuch, found their intellectual beginnings. With her extracurricular mentors she discovered Lacanian psychoanalysis, literary theory and the French School of semiotics and discourse analysis, among other subjects.

With the dawn of democracy in 1983, the Argentine military junta languished disgraced because of its loss of the war in the Malvinas Islands; this dire loss of prestige paved the way for an initial wave of public discussion on memory, human rights and the need to address crimes that had occurred in Argentina's recent past. In a historical moment in which truth and justice were topics on everyone's lips, in which public trials of the military were recently underway, and in which a truth commission had been convened that would later produce the landmark *Never Again Report* (Nunca Más, 1984), Leonor Arfuch launched her formal academic career as a professor and researcher in the Department of Sociology. By 1988, she had also been appointed as a professor of Communication in Graphic Design. Such a position might seem unusual for someone whose formation was largely influenced by discourse analysis, sociology, language and theory. Yet all of that background served to fuel hybrid, creative, interdisciplinary thinking, something that was particularly noteworthy in a political environment that, by that time, was marked by conservative backlash. We can't forget that the late 1980s and the entire decade of the 1990s were characterized by the privatization of industry, the advancement of neoliberalism and the curtailment of much of the progress that had been made to that point in the areas of truth, justice and reparations for the dictatorship's victims; this same period also saw the approval of Argentina's 'Full Stop' (Ley de Punto Final) and 'Due Obedience' (Ley de Obediencia Debida) laws, which essentially put an end to the possibility of trials until the mid-2000s.[2] In that context, Arfuch championed the design of the 'Cultural Critique' course at UBA, which pioneered the idea that critiques of visual communication, art and graphic design could be applied to the study of areas as diverse as education, communication and memory. These new approaches – and the emergence of cultural critique as a unique mode of inquiry that could be deployed to unpack the complex relationships among politics, aesthetics, ethics and society – impacted an entire generation of students and faculty and left an indelible mark on the tenor of Argentine intellectual life from that moment onwards.

Arfuch's earliest critical work was born in the time of 'democratic spring', a time that, in her own words, saw the 'semiotic opening of physical meeting places in the city: the street, the plaza, cafés, tables on the sidewalk, and bookstores'.[3] It was a time in which many voices that had once been silenced re-emerged and began to be heard again: voices of Argentinians who had lived for years in exile or of those who had survived torture or suffered first-hand in the country's vast network of detention centres. This cacophony of voices spoke in genres ranging from *testimonios* to memoirs to interviews (both in the written press and on television or the radio), revealing intimate aspects of experience that gave substance and depth to Argentinians' understanding of history and attuned them to the many challenges that lay ahead.

From a young age, Arfuch had been fascinated by journalism – in fact, in the mid-1960s she thought she might become a journalist. That early passion never left her and perhaps inspired her first two major works, *La interioridad pública* (*Public Intimacy*, 1992) and *La entrevista: una invención dialógica* (*The Interview: A Dialogic Invention*, 1995), both of which engage the 'return of the subject' that dominated the social sciences in the 1980s.[4] Specifically, Arfuch fixed her critical gaze on how this 'return of the subject' took shape in dialogue with public narratives around the economy, human rights and democracy in post-dictatorship Argentina. Her reflections on the interview as a 'speech genre', in the Bakhtinian sense, gave us the first ever, comprehensive, semiotic and interdisciplinary study to probe the dynamics of the interview: its interlocutors, its power differentials, its silences, its hidden meanings, stagings and performative aspects. In short, the interview appears in Arfuch as an *intersubjective genre*, a dialogic form in which the self acknowledges the other as radical difference and in which responsibility and ethics (or the lack thereof) play key mediating roles.

Arfuch's early work on subjectivity, intersubjectivity and ethics set the stage for a major expansion of her inquiry into first-person genres that would follow on the heels of her first two books. That expansion led her to coin a critical concept that has now become the centrepiece of her work and has gained her notoriety throughout Latin America and beyond: the *biographical space*.

In her seminal book of 2002, *El espacio biográfico: dilemas de la subjetividad contemporánea* (*The Biographical*

Space: Dilemmas of Contemporary Subjectivity), Arfuch examines the place of the subject and the role of biographical and autobiographical genres within contemporary culture, arguing that such forms of expression, which range from interviews, autobiographies, memoirs and *testimonios* to talk shows, reality shows, subjective documentary films, social media and *autoficciones*, are part of the structure of feeling of the contemporary era and have proliferated to such an extreme that they can be understood as both symptomatic of and contributors to a reconfiguration of subjectivity itself.[5] She holds that the contemporary ubiquity of private and intimate histories can be read, in part, as a countervailing force to the impersonalizing dynamics of market logics in the neoliberal era. Autobiographical genres are thus not simply an exercise in self-representation or self-aggrandizement but instead harbour an intersubjective dimension that is crucial to acknowledge. The *I* who speaks and shares his or her intimate life wants to be read, heard and validated by another; and the *other* who reads or watches the autobiographical act discovers in the narrative possible points of identification and disidentification.

Yet autobiographical genres are not simply meant to be read transparently. Instead, critics such as Arfuch, in dialogue with others like Philippe Lejeune, Paul de Man and Sylvia Molloy, have argued that they should be interpreted and deconstructed, their framing mechanisms assessed, their temporalities obviated and their authors even desacralized.[6] Autobiographical genres, including those that border on fiction in a more obvious sense, thus become spaces in which the singularity of experience opens onto the collective in ways that allow reflection on the ethical, narrative, political and aesthetic dimensions not only of the act of self-representation but also of life itself. Put differently, the biographical space invites an 'intimacy between strangers', as Michael Holroyd has suggested, that occurs when the *I* of autobiography resonates with or in the *other* and generates diverse reactions ranging from intimacy, affective ties, empathy and solidarity to outright rejection or abhorrence.[7]

The potent idea of the *biographical space* permeates Arfuch's *oeuvre* and is indeed a foundational concept (and even a starting point) for understanding the essays contained in *Memoria y autobiografía: exploraciones en los límites* (2013), the first of her books to be translated into English.[8] Consider, for example, the following passage:

> But here, in the genres discussed, there is something extra that Bakhtin called *biographical value*: that thing which, in every story, every attempt to give – verbal or audio-visual – form to a life questions both the narrator and narratee with respect to their own existence in terms of ethics, aesthetics and, we might even say, politics. That ephemeral communion, that virtual tuning-in, is what surely feeds the constant desire to glimpse 'real lives', while being aware of how vain that desire is, how intangible that reality, how inevitably fictional the whole story.[9]

The passage reveals a key insight that guides Arfuch's thinking: that all autobiographical acts are, in a sense, fictional. They are self-figurations that imply a putting into form that, in turn, necessarily invites critical analysis.

The 'biographical space', as a concept, has far-ranging consequences that extend both backwards and forwards in time. Its roots lie in the birth of the modern subject, which critics like Arfuch have often equated with the publication of Jean-Jacques Rousseau's *Confessions* (1766), a book that introduced readers to the internal dynamics of a first-person narrator struggling to expose the intimate aspects of his life and emotions but who spoke with sincerity and sought points of identification with readers. Mindful of this history, Arfuch sees in contemporary first-person manifestations, those of our own times, a straying away from the sincerity of the original Rousseauian gesture; instead of an easy conflation between the author and the 'character' on the page, she understands the first-person as a ubiquitous presence in our daily lives, capable not only of narcissistic self-fashioning but also of an ability to form alliances of solidarity with a range of imagined interlocutors. The subject who speaks the word *I* is not a coherent whole but rather a series of fractured, multiple selves engaged in a 'search for intimacy [with another] in the face of anonymity and the uniformity of everyday life'.[10] The subject's demand for self-realization in a moment in which collective political projects have foundered or find themselves under constant threat from countervailing political forces begs questions about the responsibility that *I* have to *You* and that *You* have to *Me*. We are constantly bombarded by stories of precarious lives, of lives that struggle to matter, to be seen and heard. How we respond when faced with those precarious lives – whether we'll identify or disidentify with them, value them or shut them out – is an ethical challenge that Arfuch raises for her readers, in line with other contemporary thinkers like Judith Butler who also understand the first-person utterance through the lens of multiplicity and intersociality.[11]

Intersubjectivity is not only a key theme in Arfuch's work but also an integral part of her own life and intellectual trajectory. On the one hand, her thinking dialogues with particular intellectual genealogies in which her work is inscribed (e.g. Mikhail Bakhtin, Philippe Lejeune, Walter Benjamin, Paul Ricoeur, Roland Barthes and others), while on the other hand it finds inspiration in (and inspires) certain contemporaries with whom she has long shared close affinities and conversations – *sus compañeras y compañeros de ruta*. Many names come to mind, among them Ernesto Laclau, Chantal Mouffe, Judith Butler, Nelly Richard, Beatriz Sarlo, Doreen Massey and Nicolás Casullo, as well as contemporary artists such as the Chilean visual artists Alfredo Jaar and Nury González and the Argentine film-maker Albertina Carri, whose works she has examined in depth. In fact, some of Arfuch's earliest articles on art and memory appeared in Beatriz Sarlo's journal *Punto de Vista* (*Point of View*, Argentina) and Nelly Richard's *Revista de Crítica Cultural* (*Journal of Cultural Critique*, Chile), two publications that served as barometers and pioneering spaces for post-dictatorship debate in the Southern Cone; they tackled topics such as the fierce battles over memory, the paucity of truth in the post-dictatorship, the role of art and literature, the challenges of *testimonio*, the lack of justice and the urgent need for a deepening of democracy. Several chapters in this book continue and broaden these discussions on memory, particularly Arfuch's valiant reflection on the controversial case of Óscar del Barco, a former Argentinian revolutionary from the 1970s whose writings in the early 2000s unleashed bitter debates among militants and intellectuals about both the memory and legitimacy of armed struggle (chapter 5).

In recent years, Arfuch has dedicated much of her writing to the subject of art and memory, attentive to the forms that representations of human suffering have taken in contexts ranging from the Holocaust to Chile, Argentina and the US–Mexico border. Sceptical of sutured, transparent narratives that tend to close off meaning – in critical affinity with her colleague and friend Nelly Richard in Chile – Arfuch has paid special attention to films, art installations and literary works that take distance from direct (sacrosanct) experience and suffering and that approach it in ways that allow the spectator or reader to be interpellated by the text or the image rather than alienated by them. In other words, she is specifically attuned to art that questions us and puts signs into play in ways that don't ossify meaning. Even when she analyses works whose enunciation occurs in the first-person singular, it seems to be less the first-person singular that interests her than the possibility that an intimate life story might open a chance for the *other* to become involved or questioned. This perhaps explains her critical affection for works like Chilean artist Alfredo Jaar's *Geometría de la conciencia* (*Geometry of the Conscience*, analysed in chapter 7), in which a spectator, enclosed in a dark room, confronts an infinite prism of unnamed faces of victims of tragedies from around the world and wonders what his or her relationship to and responsibility for those disappeared/reappeared faces might be. Are they the faces of precarious lives that we don't wish to see or that are too painful to acknowledge? And what relationship do those faces bear to us and to one another? Through what mechanisms, power differentials and dynamics are the transhistorical genocides and tragedies of the contemporary world linked to one another or unique in their specificity?

Like Alfredo Jaar's work, which moves freely from one geography to another – naming, questioning and critiquing – Leonor Arfuch's pen moves with equal freedom and a deeply poetic prose. This is evident on every page of *Memory and Autobiography*. The book the reader has in hand is not a collection of standard academic papers but rather a series of essays in cultural critique, texts in which images and metaphors as well as rhetorical questions open spaces to interrogate the reader, much like the polyvalent works of art, literature and film that serve as the author's objects of inquiry.

Arfuch's writing is transdisciplinary, indisciplined and fluid. It seeks correspondences and probes humanity's and society's open wounds, weaving metaphor upon metaphor and illuminating both the traps and releases of language and form. It's clear that Arfuch is inspired by Walter Benjamin's method of opening debate through juxtaposition and dialogue (what she calls 'digression as method', *el rodeo como método*), a way of surrounding the object of inquiry, blanketing it, testing it, to open it up and illuminate it.[12] In this way, she creates a constellation of images and words that speak volumes about the contemporary world, moving from the Holocaust (in her analysis of the French artist Christian Boltanski's work) to the polyphonic testimony of five female survivors of the ESMA concentration camp in Argentina, to the troubled borderlands between Tijuana and San Diego. In her analysis of the ESMA survivors' testimonial act, Arfuch illuminates the complex relationship between trauma and autobiography and thinks in dialogue with feminist intellectuals such as Leigh Gilmore and Sidonie Smith.[13]

Arfuch's most extensive chapter (chapter 2) creatively juxtaposes Boltanski's work on the Shoah with Holroyd's reflections on life writing and the work of the famed German novelist and resident of England, W. G. Sebald (1944–2001), taking us on a historical and poetic journey through Sebald's Norwich. Chapter 3 expands the discussion of these same authors, this time by evoking Sebald's main character in *Austerlitz* (2001), who goes by a 'name that is not his own', as well as Boltanski's 1989 art installation titled *Storage Area of the Children's Museum*, which features racks piled with children's clothing, an image that recalls the sheer magnitude of the disaster and the way in which the Shoah stripped its victims of their individuality, identity and dignity. The reference to Sebald evokes the 10,000 orphans who arrived at Liverpool Street Station in London (1938–1939) escaping Nazi persecution. Placed in conversation, these references allude – transnationally, transhistorically, elliptically – to the case of the children stolen by the military and their supporters during Argentina's most recent dictatorship. Today, these children are adults who struggle to recover their true identities, aided in their quest by the Grandmothers of Plaza de Mayo. In each of these instances, Arfuch shows how artists rescue singular bits of memory and experience, *naming* phenomena that would assuredly otherwise be relegated to the dustbin of history. In so doing, she allows us to understand not only how difficult it is to represent past trauma and violence – to *name* experience – but also how vitally necessary it is to do so as a political strategy for combating the tides of forgetting and for finding ways of being in common. Art and memory, like the 'biographical space', become possible strategies for building community where it has been torn asunder by greed, power and violence.

Children of dictatorship who struggle to reconstruct their traumatic pasts, torture survivors, leftist militants trying to make sense of their participation in the armed struggle of the 1970s, migrants excluded from place and territory, history's forgotten: these are the protagonists of *Memory and Autobiography*, the voices and experiences that Arfuch dignifies and explores through her writing. Writing as an act of debt, writing as an act of thought and inquiry, writing as an act of resistance, writing as an act of justice where there is no justice, writing as an elusive framing of the grey zones of human experience: all of these senses converge in Leonor Arfuch's own critical-biographical space, one that invites us into a conversation, into a community, to share in the pleasure and pain of the text and to be transformed by it.

Michael J. Lazzara

Prologue

This book was, before any form of exploration, a promise: the hope of being able to respond to questions swirling around a heteroclite set that could be summed up by an abstract, inclusive signifier: narratives from the recent past.

Narratives that in the diversity of their registers – writing, films, debates, performances, visual artworks – displayed, with symptomatic insistence, the peremptory mark of a past like an open wound, whose urgency came to light, as Benjamin might express it, in voices, images, polemics and gestures. Cries and whispers.

A symbolic plot in which the self-referential undoubtedly predominates, in a range that extends from canonical forms of testimony, memories, biography and autobiography, interviews, life stories or trajectories to hybrid, interstitial forms that at times cross generic boundaries or the thresholds of the personal: autofictions, notebooks, prison diaries, letters, agendas, obituaries, photographs, memoirs. The voices of the victims of the dictatorship in Argentina (1976–1983), of children of the disappeared, of former militants, of those living in exile, of witnesses, of authors who question themselves about their ancestors, of intellectuals who stir their memories, of inquisitive youths, of creative individuals who opt for lyric, allegorical or experimental modes, of thinkers who re-examine lost paths, utopias and disillusions ...

While a growing immersion in (one's own) subjectivity is undoubtedly a sign of the times, it nevertheless acquires other connotations when that subjective expression is articulated elliptically, declaratively, even militantly, to the problematic horizon of the collective. An articulation that is not always clear-cut, that, as a theoretical concern, skirts any evocation of 'the collective' – memory, the imaginary, representations, identities – and, therefore, particularly merits analysis. So these questions arose: What is the distance between *I* and *We*, or rather, a 'tenuous "we"', as Judith Butler would say?[1] How can biography and memory be linked in those narratives? What (varied, masked) forms does auto/biography adopt there? How does the story configure experience? And where does the boundary lie between testimony and fiction?

These questions suggested a possible route for my research, which from the first posited a negation of pre-set limits – discursive genres, spaces, fields of knowledge, artistic expressions; it was, instead, a journey through frontier zones, an openness to dialogue, to conversation, to unexpected trajectories. Given that constellation of dissimilar forms and aesthetics, my idea was to attempt to identify certain recurrent figures in the imaginary, (social) bonds of affection, in short, the diverse ways in which that traumatic trace of the events is inscribed in individual destinies, and so to find, from the perspective of cultural criticism, certain interpretive keys to a *situated subjectivity* in aesthetic, ethical and political terms.

Far from any pretension to *representativeness*, the selection of corpus to be analysed was arbitrary and random, the product of the conjunction of readings, journeys, films, museum visits, exhibitions, close encounters and conversations. The voice, the act of listening and the gaze became essential elements. Rather than investigating *memory* – safely in the realm of the established singular – I was interested in the 'unforgetful' as Nicole Loraux[2] so happily expresses it, that active piercing, performative thing capable of shaping and subverting the story, of appearing without being called up in a simple conversation, in a here-and-now that coexists with an everyday state of affairs still to emerge, still to show its face, forming part of both a shared history and each individual life. The fact is that we have been living, here or in other places, in the sadness of exile, a 'poetics of distance',[3] or in interior exile, in a threatened ordinariness, a state of exception that, over the years, gradually became naturalized routine. During that time – a lifetime that cannot be placed in parenthesis – some of us continued to carry out the rituals of 'normal life', while other lives were completely abnormal. That ordinariness of the 'outside', of every step being an equal risk, of knowing and not knowing – one of the strategies of disappearance – also formed part of my study.

There was then, in scenes involving present bodies – an ideal of communication – a particular disposition to listen to what wanted to come to light from the past: fear, emotion, experience, the painful imprint. The story then opens and closes like a lightning bolt. As in truth we always live in a routine of gestures, voices and journeys, with the whole of the past under our skin and on the surface of language, only to be suddenly woken for moments, perhaps by another voice, by some circumstance, by a meeting. And then what is spoken closes up again in order to live on, but changed. Every story transforms the lived experience, gives it further nuances. Maybe another meaning. Every story also notes a difference in the trajectory of the world. It inscribes something that was not there before. Something that never ceases to emerge. That is why all closure sounds authoritarian. If it is now time to not speak, to stem the flow of the voice. To place the numbered books on the shelf of history. To move on. Experience tells us that although there are temporalities of memory, the stories never finish. And there are things that cannot be spoken and cannot perhaps initially be heard in the first moments of a voice. But can be heard later. By other ears and another form of listening. And when I speak of the voice, I am not excluding the gaze: that story the image tells us, that place where art – with poetry – takes its greatest gambles.

Possibly for that reason, for how metaphor can work on evils, *misfortunes*, as the Ancient Greeks would say, other voices and images, other spaces and other languages were incorporated into my reflections: literatures, biographies, artistic practices, memories from other times and the ill-starred present: that place where we can share pain and loss, whatever the motive for the suffering. A place that is protected from media subjugation and commiseration, where *digression*, also a Benjaminian method, imposes a poetic, ethical, aesthetic distance on the narrative: voices on voices, allegories, metonyms, a say/show that recognizes the Barthesian notion of delicacy and that is aware of the limits of the inexpressible.

So, after journeying around the places that make up a personal biography, however unaware one might be of them – the *poetics of space*, as Bachelard[4] would say – the work of the notable German writer Sebald and of the French visual artist Christian Boltanski, both of whom were marked by the memory imprint of the war and the Shoah, came into dialogue in chapter II, 'The Gaze as Autobiography: Time, Place, Objects'. To these voices is added that of Michael Holroyd, the well-known English biographer, who speaks of the task of giving *form* to a life that didn't exist before the narrative.[5] Memory and autobiography are woven here in a variety of ways, producing a precise image of the imprint of the collective on the individual, according to the existential arc of each life. The dilemmas of representation, the signi-fying – and even dazzling – quality of form, the tension between the singular and the number – the atrocious number of losses – are also included in this dialogue.

In the following chapter, 'Memory and Image', Sebald and Boltanski meet again in two contrasting scenes – one literary, the other visual – where a scene from Sebald's *Austerlitz*[6] contains both the key to the novel and a heart-rending real-life story – one of many still coming to light more than half a century after the end of the war – and, in my view, finds its obverse in Boltanski's characteristically allegorical reference to the Shoah, *Storage Area of the Children's Museum*,[7] an installation the artist donated to the Musée d'art Moderne de la Ville de Paris. Here the mystery of an origin – Sebald's character, someone who only knows that the name he goes by is not his own – and the restlessness of an incessant quest in which the sudden flowering of memory provokes the glimmer of a revelation are disturbingly close echoes of the stories of the stolen children of Argentina searching for their true identities.[8]

Chapter 4, 'Women Who Narrate: Autobiography and Traumatic Memories', contains an analysis of those signifiers in *That Inferno: Conversations of Five Women Survivors of*

an Argentine Torture Camp, a book co-authored by Munú
Actis, Cristina Aldini, Liliana Gardella, Miriam Lewin and
Elisa Tokar,[9] as well as in Pilar Calveiro's doctoral thesis.[10]
What interests me in these texts recounting similar experiences are the different perspectives offered by two contrasting
enunciative positions (the narrative/autobiographical *I* in
the former, the third person in the latter) and their consequences at discursive, ethical and political levels. Through
an analysis of discourse, I attempt to demonstrate not
only what the narrators do with language but also, and
more importantly, *what language does with them*, using
a performative conception with a focus on gender. I also
attempt to contribute a possible ethics of discursive genres to
the discussion on testimony.

The well-known 'del Barco debate', which some years ago
provoked great interest among intellectuals and academics
and gave rise to a prolific circulation of letters that were later
collected in two volumes,[11] is the focus of chapter 5, 'Political
Violence, Autobiography and Testimony'. Over and above
the conflicting arguments, which form an almost inextricable
plot, I was particularly interested in the *biographical* slant
they assume, the way theoretical and/or political positions
and lived experience interconnect and overlap (at times with
uncommon virulence). In this way, by listening to the *tones*
of the debate, I proposed to read them as a symptom. As
symptomatic of the state of the soul – if I can be permitted
this expression – of the political left in Argentina – in all its
diversity – and the huge difficulty of analysing the chiaro-
scuro of the recent past.

In the following chapter, 'The Threshold, the Frontier:
Explorations at the Limits', the limits of the exploration are
literally extended to one of the 'hot frontiers' of the planet: the
Tijuana/San Diego border, an emblematic, militarized point
on the troubled line dividing Mexico and the United States.
What takes me there are artistic interventions that show
the potential of public art and critical art – the definition of
which is also discussed in this chapter – for revealing present
suffering, the type that is produced on a daily basis in a world
that has accepted living in conditions of perpetual warfare,
of growing violence and inequality. Physical frontiers increasingly concerned with expulsion rather than reception deny

the glory of global connectivity. Within this section, there is a proposal related to the issue of territoriality, to the difficulty of recognition, to other memories from recent pasts, with their victims and disappearances, plus an evaluation of art's ethical commitment in terms of communication and *translation*, as modes of stimulating Bakhtin's 'dialogic principle',[12] a possibility that is expressed in the works of the artists selected for analysis: Antoni Muntadas, Krzysztof Wodiczko, Francis Alÿs and Alfredo Jaar.

The final chapter, 'The Name, the Number' brings together the strands of the journey in a reflection on the ethical imprint of the *name*, constantly masked by the numbers of victims seen – even if inadvertently – on screens, just as the name was covered up in diverse recent pasts, from the Shoah to the last military dictatorship in Argentina, where the number replaced the name of detainees as a first step to their disappearance. I then consider the relationship between name and number as it appears in the works of Sebald and Boltanski, in relation to the story of the survivors of the ESMA,[13] and in intellectual debate to then proceed to other works of public art by Krzysztof Wodiczko and Alfredo Jaar, which, like an Aleph, embody the majority of the questions posed in this book, and where the name assumes the sense of a restoration of humanity. The chapter closes with an evocation of the 'wall of names' – or Monument to the Victims of State Terrorism – in the Parque de la Memoria, here in Buenos Aires.

Backtracking to my opening chapter, 'A Beginning' synthesizes the transdisciplinary theoretical perspective of my research.

If the selection of authors that accompany this journey was marked by the poetic and metaphorical development of their verbal or visual works and by digression as a method, which can be recognized in all of them, I now, at the end of this long exploration, realize that this method also marked my own work: distance from the immediate and painful, voices over voices, memories over memories, and an attempt to offer vulnerability the shelter of the word, without losing heart, with the hope – possibly shared with critical art – that this narrative has, returning to Benjamin, managed to produce justice.

1

A Beginning

Being at the limit: these words do not yet form a proposition, and even less a discourse. But there is enough in them, provided that one plays upon it, to engender almost all the sentences in this book.

Jacques Derrida (1982)

It is with these mysterious, thought-provoking words that Derrida begins 'Tympan', the first chapter of *Margins of Philosophy*,[1] in both graphic and metaphorical counterpoint to a parallel, marginal text by Michel Leiris that, over the pages, speaks of curves, helicoids, spirals, snails, those natural and symbolic simulations of the ear and, therefore, the act of *hearing*, as philosophy's impulse towards *différence*, the multiplicity of (also marginal) sounds and voices; in short, the refutation of the margin as marginality and decentralization in order to place it in *opposition*, in terms of a fully inhabited space, to the supposed centrality of philosophy as a founding discourse and the illusion of *presence* in that centre.

Given this incitement, it may be possible to see in the apparent centrality of the subject in contemporary culture, in its pre-eminence within the duplicitous splitting of the ego, in those biographical indications to be found in every type of discourse – from the most canonical to the most innovative; from classic autobiography to autofiction, from the intimate diary to the blog – a proliferation of voices striving to be heard, disputing ethical, aesthetic and political spaces, subverting the imprecise limits of the private and the public, and also making the distinction between centre and margin impossible to articulate.

Some time ago, the notion of the 'return of the subject' was celebrated in theories of difference and perceived – from another viewpoint – as the decline of public culture and the primacy of the social. Over the intervening years, this prominence has been increasingly asserted in the media, academic research and artistic experimentation without, however, being disconnected from other notions of sociality. Faces, voices, bodies take over the role of words; they sustain authorships, reaffirm positions of agency or authority, testify to having lived or having seen; they bare their emotions and underpin the politics of identity. It is a phenomenon which tends to be defined as the extension – or even removal – of the limits of 'biographical space',[2] the 'subjective turn'[3] or a late effect of those 'transformations of intimacy'[4] that will lead to speaking without euphemism of 'public intimacy'.[5]

Nevertheless, this often-excessive subjectivism – which can also include the expansion of the self-help genre – does not position the subject – the multiplicity of subjects – at centre stage. Conversely, that centre – whether termed the market, global capitalism or the metaphysical moment that regulates world stock markets, causing them to rise or fall at will – presents itself with no recognizable face, *no subject*, as the blind power behind mere puppets, defining the trends imposed on those who execute that will in their capacity as heads of governments, regions or international organizations, in which the tension between politics (as an administrative routine) and *the political* (the agonistic struggle for hegemony) generally settles in favour of the former.[6]

It is perhaps in exact counterpoint to this hypothetical centre (and its entropy), resistant to any adjectival qualification attempting to attenuate its devastating effects (what would a humane capitalism look like?), that the overwhelming emergence of subjectivity should be read, those small stories that – according to some – have substituted the grand narratives whose decline was foretold more than two decades ago by the controversial concept of postmodernity, the decline of the collective subjects that commemorations establish in the space of nostalgia – the fortieth anniversary of May 1968, for example – whose comparison to the present, with its unblemished individualism, is a constant source of deception.

Small stories we can *hear* – pricking up our ears in a sense given by Derrida – even in the silence of writing, in the testimony related to a traumatic shared memory in the story of a life offered to the researcher as the emblematic feature of the social, in the *subjective documentary* (no longer an oxymoron but a new genre), in the artistic installations composed of intimate objects, in theatre as *biodrama* or in images (often without voice) of catastrophes and suffering that the media have converted into one of the paradigmatic records of the age.

It could be argued that this heteroclite list does not do justice to the valuative differences between genres – testimony or life story as opposed to media sensationalism, for example; experimentation in writing and the visual arts as opposed to the explosion of the personal on the Web – but the truth is that – without any wish to asperse the pertinence of that venture – my gaze is not so much directed at the hierarchical ordering of the discursive genres involved in this reconfiguration of contemporary subjectivity as at the reconfiguration in itself in symptomatic terms.

But why the reconfiguration? What would be new – and symptomatic – about that tendency if there have always been self-referential voices, if the narration of a life can possibly be traced back to the distant ancestors of folk tales? In response to these questions, three signifiers can be posited: historicity, simultaneity and multiplicity.

First, genres that are considered as canonical – autobiography, memoirs, the personal diary, correspondence – have a precise historicity that marks a break with an earlier time: they were consubstantial with that invention of the modern subject which is generally agreed to have come about in the eighteenth century with Jean-Jacques Rousseau's *Confessions* – the space of interiority and emotion which must be *spoken* in order to exist, the (consequent) public expression of the emotions and the restrictive weight of society on them.[7] A new sensibility, an astute – and anguished – historical consciousness accompanied the consolidation of capitalism,

the bourgeois world and its classic separation of the public
and the private. And although it is true that those genres
were never invalidated, that they were, through centuries,
affirmed and transformed, adopting other formats and
media, it was with the dizzying deployment of new communications technologies that their imprint became *global*,
recognizable everywhere in astonishing simultaneity, without
respect for physical frontiers, linguistic traditions or diverse
cultural environments. This expansion is not only due to
classic personal experience-based contents, modulated by
the complexities of our times, but is also aesthetic, stylistic,
manifested in multiple, innovative forms: autofiction, for
example, which, in contrast to classic autobiography, offers
the reader or addressee a series of equivocations, tricks,
where the boundaries between real and fictitious characters
and events are blurred; the docudrama, which also involves
an erosion of boundaries; the media confessional, which
oscillates between intimate revelation and staged spectacle;
the multiple variants of the reality show; the online lives of
social media ...

In the configuration of the symptomatic horizon, a number
of factors come into play: a patent simultaneity linked to
a journalistic emphasis on voice and *presence*, particularly
in the interview, also a highly important genre of social
research;[8] an insistence on the figure of the speaker as a
guarantor of authenticity – an *I* and another *I*, there is no
substantial difference – and which even extends to creators
of fiction;[9] the temptation to reveal intimate details and the
corresponding passion for glimpsing them; and, finally, the
incessant multiplication of persons and characters from the
famous – of every sphere – to ordinary people.

There are, therefore, different types of subjects on the
margins: literally – in both senses of the word – in those
inscriptions left by a nervous hand on the blank border of the
manuscript[10]; in the crossings-out that mark the halting steps
of inspiration; in the notebooks from childhood or travels,
which, while lacking the rhetoric of a personal diary, have a
close relationship to it; in the rediscovered papers,[11] or those
conserved in literary archives; in the secret correspondence
that comes to light ...[12] and even in postcards registering
the fleeting trace of a landscape. It may be that never before

have these texts, snippets of interiority, of thought or lived experience, given rise to such editorial enthusiasm, an enthusiasm they share with other sacred species: biographies, autobiographies, compilations of interviews, testimonies, memoirs ...,[13] as shown by the bestseller lists of any cultural scenario.

There is no doubt that, in the characteristic tonality of this discursive space (using discourse in the widest acceptation given by Wittgenstein as word, image, gesture, way of life[14]), 'biographical value' is of prime importance since it 'is capable of organizing not only the story of another person's life, but also the experiencing of life itself and the story of one's own life; it can be the form in which one gains consciousness of one's own life, the form in which one sees and gives utterance to one's own life'.[15] A number of aspects of this concept that perhaps best explain the predominance of biography in contemporary society deserve to be foregrounded. First, its intersubjectivity, the possibility of fomenting an understanding between the narrator and the addressee with respect to both the experience of 'one's own life' and 'the experiencing of life itself', that is to say, the ethical dimension of life in general. Second, its quality of *form*, a construction of (narrative, expressive) form that is also a construction of meaning, a *form of comprehension*. Biographical values are, then, 'values that are shared in common by life and art' and are capable of defining practical acts; 'they are the form and values of an *aesthetic of lived life*'.[16]

Following this idea, and taking into account that the story of a life implies temporality, there also exists within the biographical space something that could be termed *memory value*, which carries the remembrance of a past, with its symbolic and often traumatic weight for the individual and/ or collective experience, into the narrative present. This is a doubly significant value when the biographical account is centred precisely on *that past* in itself, due to what it has left as a mark, as an ineradicable trace of an existence. It is a value that appears exalted in different formats, including the visual, opening the way for new turns, like certain intellectual memories that, distanced from classic autobiography, form a mesh of readings, theoretical courses and vital experiences in a unique articulation.[17]

If remembrance forms an obligatory part of the operations of the transmission of culture, of the trace of history
and the 'invention of tradition' in every society, it is from
the paradigmatic landmark of Auschwitz, the Shoah, that
the question of memory – as a dilemma and the inevitable
(theoretical, ethical, political) elaboration of the atrocities
of the twentieth century and its 'beyond'[18] – has become
one of the most important present-day registers, particularly in relation to what can be termed recent history. It has
been said that memorial inflation, to the extent that it not
only deploys numerous narratives in a deferred temporality
(personal memories, testimonies, experiences, anecdotes,
every variety of visual and documentary material) but also, in
close relationship, the official politics of memory (museums,
memorials, monuments, counter-monuments, anniversary
lists, commemorations ...) forms a material and symbolic
mechanism that can, in the words of Todorov, turn into the
'abuses of memory'.[19]

Yet it is not only the past that tortures memory (and its
obligatory 'uses of forgetting'[20]), from the terrible experience
of Nazism to the violent Latin American dictatorships of the
seventies, to give just two notable examples. Memory is also
tortured by its transfiguration in the present in the form of
a perpetual state of warfare that merely changes location in
distant, devastated environments (Iraq, Afghanistan, Gaza)
but which can unexpectedly knock on the door in the nerve
centres of large cities, categorizing as 'victim' a recurrent
figure whose identity is masked by statistics that are no
less terrifying for being abstract. If the present ascendancy
of testimony has added to the elaboration of the traumatic
experiences of past decades, so surrounding the unspeakable
with words (as is known, there are temporalities of memory,
things that can only emerge gradually as the years pass and
distance ameliorates the anguish, frees the secret or the
prohibition), it is photography that now appears to have
taken responsibility for recording the mute present suffering
experienced by whole populations. Whether it be in the press
or in art, or their ever more frequent overlapping spaces,[21]
photographers are making their images into a narrative that
is always lacking in biographical singularity. Stories versus
(heart-rending) images, whose proliferation poses not a few

ethical and aesthetic dilemmas, and which also delineate the margin of those who are on the outside: outside their native lands on forced migrations; outside a country of asylum, in refugee camps; 'of no account'[22] to those who are counting.[23]

With varying stresses, the following chapters address the relationship between biography and memory and, hence, between biographical value and memory value, plus the ways in which autobiography, autofiction, memory and testimony articulate in verbal and visual narratives that defy rigid canons. This is a terrain that gives preference to the essay, where various disciplines coexist (theories of language and discourse, visual semiotics, psychoanalysis, political theory, literary and cultural criticism), tracing out border zones that pose new questions without fear of the limits being erased.

2
The Gaze as Autobiography: Time, Place, Objects

Auto/biographical narration, as with any narrative form, appears primarily to invoke temporality, that existential arc that unfolds – and folds in on itself – from some imaginary point of commencement and passes unpredictably through the obligatory stations of life, oscillating between difference and repetition, between what tends towards shared experience and what distinguishes each trajectory. But although it may be possible to respond to the question 'How is a life narrated?' in ways that can be both diverse yet true, the issue of which places make up a biography and how emotion and place are linked is more complex. As key enquirers into the definition of biographical space, W. G. Sebald's experience in literature and Christian Boltanski's in the visual arts offer possibly unexpected – and even disturbing – replies in the ongoing task of keeping 'death in its place', as Michael Holroyd (whose voice is also heard here) puts it.[1]

Journeys: time, place

'... poetically man dwells ...' Poetry builds up the very nature of dwelling. Poetry and dwelling not only do not exclude each other; on the contrary, poetry and dwelling belong together, calling for one another.

Martin Heidegger (2001)[2]

The space of biography may well begin in the house, the home, the dwelling place, in the strongest sense of dwelling: being in the world, in addition to having shelter, protection, a refuge. The house of one's birth, as an initial point of a 'poetics of space', as Bachelard would term it,[3] a way of inhabiting the place sheltering the memory of the body and the earliest images that may not be irrecoverable and so constitute a species of mythical plinth of subjectivity – an ecstatic place in photographs guarding unique moments but also the first territory of exploration, of journeys that define the actions and inner beings of its inhabitants.

I would like to linger in this small universal landscape: the kitchen, the living room, the bedroom, the cellar and the attic. Each with its poetic and dramatic weight: laughter, celebrations around the dining table, the warmth of a lamp by the window and the shadows in the corner that give an inkling of moments of melancholy or thought. The house as space/temporality, in Doreen Massey's perception, the product of interrelationships and interactions from the immensity of the global to the intimately tiny, as the possibility of the existence of *multiplicity*, 'the sphere in which distinct trajectories coexist; as the sphere therefore of coexisting *heterogeneity*'.[4] The house, then, is composed of interactions, emotional relationships, routines, everyday comings and goings, where gender also marks its rhythms.[5]

Crossing the threshold into the public sphere, the street, neighbourhood, city – that also form a part of biographical space – we could lose ourselves with Benjamin (despite the disappearance of the *flâneur*) or 'write' those transits with Michel de Certeau, even though we may be incapable of reading them according to his own expression.[6] However, the invisibility of those transits through space – footprints at a walking pace – does not desensitize bodies, which carry their burden of repetition, the minimum of space that day after day they must dispute with the crowds. A nomadic or metaphorical city, returning to the author, which overflows the urban trace, susceptible to being thought from the poetic or mythic perspective of space.

Despite the automatism of walking through the same places, our often vacant stares as we view the fleeting landscape outside the window, we can at times evoke the steps of other times in a place where everything has changed. So we are often surprised on our return – from journeys, exile or living in another place – not to recognize the place as our own. The things that have disappeared, even when they are not ours, have taken with them something of our biography, just as the houses we no longer inhabit have become strangely other: other lights and shadows, other people dwelling there, people unaware of what those walls enclose, the intensity of bodies, gestures, emotions that endure, perhaps like energy fields.[7]

The difference between interior and exterior has a certain similarity to that of distance and proximity,[8] the panoramic view from on high and the 'below' of the multitude, the swirl of movement and respiration in the street. The immensity of the metropolis, its unimaginable vastness in the case of the megacity, leaves its human character in doubt, so giving rise to a wide variety of fantasies, from geological cataclysms to science fiction: the megacity of Sao Paulo with its mountain crest of buildings that seem to sprout uncontrolled from the earth; the infinite nocturnal plane of Los Angeles in the unforgettable images of *Blade Runner*; or the unexpected ocean of lights that is Mexico City any evening on coming down from the Ajusco lava dome.

'To walk is to lack a place', says de Certeau. 'The moving about that the city multiplies and concentrates makes the city itself an immense social experience lacking a place.'[9] But would it not be possible, on the contrary, to believe that walking is also *an appropriation of place*, just as reading or listening appropriate the text, incorporating it, transforming it into experience? Naturally, there are walks undertaken out of duty – or desperation – and others for the pleasure of ambulation. It is possible to conceive the city as a narrative textual structure, where metaphors, metonyms, hyperbole and, in particular, oxymoron are in constant articulation under the experienced gaze of the poet or critic, although they might escape the busy passer-by. It can, however, also be conceived as the 'empire of signs', to quote Roland Barthes's title,[10] where the visual – related to but not inseparable from sound (the silence of the nocturnal city) – can generate great unease. The city, then, as a place of encountering the Other in all its ethical, linguistic, cultural and sexual otherness, inhabited by names – streets, squares, neighbour-hoods, monuments, buildings, businesses – in a capricious cartography that unites transcendental historical events with remote territories, that creates a dialogue between unknown heroes and artists, poets, saints, musicians, tradespeople and herbalists, in groupings reminiscent of Borges' Chinese encyclopaedia. Those names, which we pass through time and again, also form part of biographical space. But not everything in the city has a name or can be seen. There are names and places that are inaccessible to the visual sense; even though we live in ancient spaces, the new rises up on the remains of the old, accumulations on ruins, mysteries, a blurred backdrop: we sleep where 'ancient revolutions slumber'.[11]

Literature and cinema constantly explore those mysteries of the city. In terms of cinema, the city is a protagonist in the greater part of the films we watch, the privileged scenario of all the registers of human life: people, histories, myths, relationships, sensations, violence. In this way, and through a visual impact that becomes habit, we recognize other landscapes in an anticipatory effect: on some possible journey, before arriving, we have already followed the paths of – and suffered with – innumerable characters in a strange form of familiarity. Just as, according to the old anthropological adage, after being there we are excited by its appearance on the screen, whatever the plot of the film. And the conjunction of cinema, literature and autofiction can bring about such successful experiments as Régine Robin's *Mégapolis* (2009),[12] a book with an interesting subtitle: *Les derniers pas du flâneur*, where, seeking a 'poetics of megalopolis', the narrator invites readers to accompany her as she strolls through some of them (New York, Tokyo, Los Angeles, London, Buenos Aires), following the footsteps of a number of fictional characters.

We have come a long way from the house of one's birth. The point is that, in this case, Heidegger's[13] distinction between *dwelling* and *travelling* is less clear: to dwell is also to travel, both physically and virtually, particularly in these days of *navigating* the Web (the choice of verb was not casual), with the possible loss of the capacity for abstract thought, without external references. Even today transits seem to give priority to moorings and roots – unless one thinks, as Barthes does, of 'roots in the air'.[14] That movement, which nevertheless does not discount genealogies, identifications, emotions or belongings, can also include identities in terms of narrative rather than essentialism, fluctuations between the same and the other, what remains and what changes, that constitutive otherness of oneself.[15] Consideration of the relationship between space and subjectivity – the city as autobiography – also presupposes that fluctuation, a discreet temporality of present pasts, a social and emotional mesh, configured by the experience itself, a spatiality inhabited by discontinuities that are both physical and related to memory.

But in terms of memory, how does that Aristotelian aporia of making present what is absent work? Because, according to Aristotle, when remembering, what we recall is an image and the emotion that image carries. It can, therefore, be asserted that there is no image without *place*, a spatial context, an environment in which it is located, and also, to give a Benjaminian slant, that in the city – in particular – memory comes out to meet us at every step, even when we are not expecting it. Memories of their own temporality – and then immediately historic – and memories that belong to us, that are stored, unremembered in an attic, but which suddenly appear on turning a corner, on seeing a house from another time, the location of a happy or unhappy moment ... unexpected images that speak in an unpredictable syntax.

Between the distant, historical memory of events and people we may not know, whose trace in space has not attracted our attention, and familiar, biographical memory that invests places and moments in time with an emotional response, there are other memories from recent pasts that insistently, painfully, remain in the collective conscience. Memories linked to traumatic events, whose physical, material moorings also confront the pedestrian but not so unexpectedly: extant traces, inscriptions, plaques, tombstones, museums, monuments, memorials. Urban markers signalling suffering and tragic fates, war wounds, disappearances, xenophobia, persecution.

But it is not only urban space that stores the marks of the past, the spectral forms of those who came before, the voices that were once heard in the places we now inhabit. The road, the countryside, forests and stones also bear witness for those who know how to question them, how to *make them speak*. This is what W. G. Sebald, the German author considered to be one of the greatest of contemporary writers, does so brilliantly: his work is an answer to the question of which places make up a biography. On the road, on a journey, wandering through deserted lands or emblematic sites, in one might say an almost entomological relationship with a harsh natural world, downtrodden by the passing of centuries.

In *The Rings of Saturn*,[16] the narrator, identified with the biographical voice, decides to take a walking tour of the public footpaths of Suffolk in the east of England – the country in which he lived for more than thirty years until his death in 2001. Suffolk is an area of great beauty, with forests, rolling countryside and a coastline of summer resorts that look across to the mainland of the continent. The county is unusual in that it has no cities, only towns and villages, some of them sleeping in time, with oblique traces of a past that is hard to imagine. Nevertheless, Sebald's writing – the writing of his character – transforms this walking tour into a fascinating adventure which brings together nature and history, description and conjecture, people and biographies, in a profundity of experience that configures a new territory for autobiography: it is the gaze, the declared actuality of presence, that returns the imprint of historicity to the natural environment and the various stages of the journey, the event in the imaginary process of the development of a happening, in the scene that is recreated before the eyes in vivid tones under the inspiration of dream or pictorial images, of photographs, several of which accompany the text. A scene inhabited by voices whose shown heterogeneity,[17] as Jacqueline Authier[18] would term it, not only restores a polyphonic echo of diverse authorships (stories, archives, images, anecdotes, overheard conversations) but also clothes them affectively – poetically – in the cadence and modulation of the voice itself.[19]

That singular gaze is capable of perceiving, from a deserted beach, the noise of a fierce sea battle that took place centuries before, of imagining the movements and feelings of long-past inhabitants, deciphering forgotten inscriptions, reading the marks of splendorous pasts in the trace of a garden overgrown with weeds, or in the tangled mass of the crowns of trees. It is even capable of recreating, in the poetics of the enunciation itself, old descriptions of illustrious places, such as Somerleyton Hall, which he visited during his tour:

> Below, you see the steep roofs tiled with dark blue slate, and in the snow-white glow from the shimmering glasshouses the level blackness of the lawns. Further off in the park drift the shadows of Lebanese cedars; in the deer enclosure, the wary animals keep an eye open in their sleep; and beyond the furthermost perimeter, away toward the horizon, the marshes extend and the sails of windmills are turning in the wind.[20]

None of this would be seen by visitors to the hall today, the narrator points out as he passes through dusty rooms and passages filled with 'bygone paraphernalia': it is a long time since it could have been said to be a *dwelling*. Yet there are familiar objects that have survived their owners which, stored in glass cases, give evidence of genealogies, customs, privileges and hobbies: portraits, golf clubs, tennis rackets, trophies from safaris, African masks, souvenirs of the inexorable passage of time and the ephemeral nature of trajectories: 'autobiographical moments'[21] that place us, as readers, in harmony with the enunciator in a reflexive, mutual relationship; they address us in our own ephemeral condition.

Those moments are accentuated in the chapters dealing with the biographical details of the eminent people who left some trace on the area through which his footsteps take him. Rigorous, encyclopaedic information – lives and works – articulate with the imaginary trace of an ordinary future, moments and scenes that may have taken place, literary or scientific trajectories read in the light of the texts that speak of them – voices over voices – with a view to the significant details that give an inkling of the passions, the emotions, the concerns of people from another time – yet without anachronism: all this in precise, perfect prose, with echoes of Borges. The journey also includes: the fabulous adventure of discovering that Thomas Browne (admired by Borges and Adolfo Bioy Casares, whose voices are also woven into the story) once lived in Norwich,[22] in the adjoining county of Norfolk, until his death in 1682; the mishaps of Joseph

Conrad, who disembarked in Lowestoft, a town the narrator
visits, linked to the extraordinary story of Roger Casement,
the first person to denounce the exterminations resulting from
colonization and slavery; the frustrated romance between
Charlotte Ives and the Viscount de Chateaubriand, who
spent some time in the village of Ilkershall, fleeing the horrors
of the French Revolution. But this journey – this writing –
that moves fluidly between eras, documents, personal diaries,
exotic places is far from being an erudite rescue mission
of the history to be found in the real places. Rather, it is a
profound work on interiority, on what, without drawing a
boundary with fiction, could perhaps most rightly be called
autobiography.

> As I sat there that evening in Southwold overlooking the
> German Ocean, I sensed quite clearly the earth's slow turning
> into the dark. The huntsmen are up in America, writes Thomas
> Browne in *The Garden of Cyrus*, and they are already past
> their first sleep in Persia. The shadow of night is drawn like a
> black veil across the earth, and since almost all creatures, from
> one meridian to the next, lie down after the sun has set, so, he
> continues, one might, in following the setting sun, see on our
> globe nothing but prone bodies, row after row, as if levelled by
> the scythe of Saturn, an endless graveyard for a humanity struck
> by falling sickness.[23]

It is no coincidence that the image of destruction, so close to a
war zone, appears in the subtle dialogue between the narrator
and his illustrious character. The image can be connected with
the author's most recondite concerns, the traumatic trace that
traverses his life and work. Autobiography – Sebald appears
to tell us – does not only refer to a personal story of vicissitudes in chronological order but is also the gaze resting on
others, the dialogues we might have with them – even after
they have disappeared – the flow of experience in time and
space. So all we are able to learn of the walker is inspired
by the path, the historical and existential coordinates that
cause him to stop in one place or another, the meeting with
classical or contemporary, real or imaginary people. And also
the piercing memories of the war, like indelible marks on the
landscape and on people. Ruins of old fortresses, camouflaged
hangars, like fossil remains, whose lethal function carries

to the present the voice of William Hazel, the gardener at
Somerleyton, as he evokes for his German visitor the nightly
shadow of British planes crossing the sky – that ancient East
Anglian sky – to bomb German cities, fortunately at some
distance from the alpine village in which Sebald was born in
May 1944.

> Every evening I watched the bomber squadrons heading out
> over Somerleyton, and night after night, before I went to sleep, I
> pictured in my mind's eye the German cities going up in flames,
> the firestorms setting the heavens alight, and the survivors rooting
> about in the ruins. One day [Lord Somerleyton] explained the
> allied bombing strategy to me, and sometime later he bought me
> a big relief map of Germany. All the place names I had heard on
> the news were marked in strange letters ...[24]

Here, in the poetic condensation of three pages, in an intense
account by the character – far distant from 'orality' – is a
foretaste of what will be the central theme of a later book
of essays, *On the Natural History of Destruction*,[25] in which
Sebald addresses the polemical topic of aerial warfare, the
bombing of the civilian populations of German cities in all
its horror. It is a text that, in the obsessive details of the
Allied operations and their consequences – where different
voices and testimonies are mingled – once again returns to
the ominous silences of the war and its extreme indignity,
and offers certain answers to my initial question of how
emotion and place are linked. Indeed, the author lingers on
that specific relationship, which appears to be idealized in
some of his compatriot's stereotypical conceptions, where the
landscape is invested with an essential identity – 'Germany'
– that survives the destruction intact. By contrast, in his
experience, at just the mention of those landscapes,

> I see pictures merging before my mind's eye – paths through
> the fields, river meadows, and mountain pastures mingling with
> images of destruction – and oddly enough, it is the latter, not
> the now entirely unreal idylls of my early childhood, that make
> me feel rather as if I were coming home [...] I now know that
> at the time, when I was lying in my bassinet on the balcony of
> the Seefeld house and looking up at the pale blue sky, there was
> a pall of smoke in the air all over Europe, over the rearguard

actions in east and west, over the ruins of the German cities, over the camps where untold numbers of people were burnt, people from Berlin and Frankfurt, from Wuppertal and Vienna from [...] Salonika and Rhodes, Ferrara and Venice – there was scarcely a place in Europe from which no one had been deported in those years.[26]

For Sebald, the traumatic memory of the war is an ongoing siege, present throughout his work, both in essays and novels, to the point that 'when I see photographs or documentary films dating from the war, I feel as if I were its child so to speak, as if those horrors that I did not experience had cast a shadow over me, and one from which I shall never entirely emerge'.[27] It is perhaps due to the constant looming shadow, the suffering he did not experience, that his mode of response to the ethical mandate – in the strongest sense given by Levinas as responding for the other and for the life of the other – is expressed in writing which distances itself from the 'facts' – without diminishing their importance – and gives preference to the voice. The voices of those who *have* lived, and suffered, and written, of those who testified to what they saw or heard or suffered, of those who succeeded in expressing it in theory or in fiction. A sensibility that is also aware of other forms of destruction: natural destruction, the inexorable passage of time on things, exhausting work, melancholy, the afflictions of the inner being.

In this way, in the final chapter of *The Rings of Saturn*, as a colophon to an erudite journey along the silk road, its oriental ancestors, the passion aroused by that precious fabric in the West and the fortunes it created in England, where the factories of Norwich were already famous before the Industrial Revolution, the narrator reflects on the work that forced workers to be strapped to machines – such as the loom – and draws a comparison between those weavers and 'scholars and writers'. Alluding to a German *Journal of Experimental Psychology* published around the time,[28] where the silk weavers' tendency to melancholy is mentioned as a mental illness, he finds a certain logic – and similarity – in work that 'forced them to sit bent over, day after day, straining to keep their eyes on the complex patterns they created',[29] a possibly reverse definition of the task of writing.

'It is difficult to imagine the depths of despair into which those can be driven who, even after the end of the working day, are engrossed in their intricate designs and who are pursued, into their dreams, by the feeling that they have got hold of the wrong thread.'[30]

With his unique way of bringing together apparently distant things, the narrator/storyteller turns once again from the familiar territory of Norwich to Germany, this time to remember a perhaps little-known episode: Hitler's 1936 project to make his country independent in relation to textile manufacture, including that of silk, resulting in the development of sericulture – related to social hygiene and other purges – the stages of which are shown in an old film. The story and the long walking tour close on 13 April 1995 with a list of the unhappy events that had occurred on that date in the fifty years since the end of the war.

The comparison with the silk weavers coincides with a style that weaves its own figures in the warp and weft of those other voices, fleshes them out, gives them depth. And if certain topics, as he said in interviews, referring to the concentration camps, can only be addressed indirectly, through second-hand accounts – stories of stories – neither can autobiography, Sebald suggests, be deployed in the mere self-satisfaction of the ego. Indeed, in both cases – and in their singular combination in the texts dealt with here – it is not merely a matter of stylistic choice, the masterful handling of reported speech. What is decisively at play here is the issue of representation, its dilemma: how to speak – of others, of oneself; which traumatic zones can be allowed to enter the disputes of discourse; how to translate horror into words; in what places the voice is silenced or hampered. So *The Rings of Saturn*, whose subtitle is *An English Pilgrimage* – a book that resists inclusion in traditional categories and is perhaps content, as Sebald himself often used to say, to be considered prose – contains metaphorical digressions, allegories, allusions, forms that sift the features of observation and imagination noted by the walker, the sudden memory that flies through time and place and the voices that he gathers together when walking, when telling stories. The narrator, the storyteller – a character who, as happens also in life, develops as he meets other characters – allows us to accompany him, trusting in his closeness to the author but without the convention of the 'autobiographical pact',[31] that is, without the promise of identity (sealed by the name) and referential adaptation, safe from the chronological minutia, on the border between reality and fiction.

Objects, memory

So many things!
Nail files, doorways, atlases, glasses, keys,
our tacit, strangely silent slaves.
They will last beyond our forgetting,
and never know that we have gone.

Jorge Luis Borges[32]

Biography, as the irruption of images *of* or *into* a place, places as the obligatory scenarios of a biography and the memory of objects have all been widely dealt with in cinema in more or less explicit terms. Jean-Luc Godard is perhaps the best example, particularly his 'self-portrait' *JLG/JLG*[33] which, expressly renouncing anecdote, is based on the poetic and metaphysical articulation of images, where metaphorical contrast has precedence over any form of referentiality. Places, corners of the houses he inhabits, phrases, quotations, allusions, landscapes, a signifying weave where interiority is refracted in the work itself in disdain of all narrative temporality, in the fusion of the instant and memory, as illustrated by the potential of experience as defined in the philosophical tradition: the intense impact of the instant and that enduring thing that resists the routine course of life.[34] As with *Roland Barthes by Roland Barthes*[35] – a recurrent model in autobiographical fiction[36] – it is precisely in the fragment, the displacement of the point of view, the landscape of the world that unfolds before the eyes (with an invitation from the camera to follow it) that the *I* of the narrator is expressed: it is the work that speaks, not the author. Or, as Paul de Man suggests in his seminal essay 'Autobiography as De-facement',[37] at the limit, all writing is autobiography. Another creator, this time from the field of the visual arts, would perhaps agree with that idea: the French 'post-conceptual' artist Christian Boltanski, who, eschewing any form of biographism, experiments with autofiction in some of his works. Here, the figure of the I fades into other people or carries out that 'positioning oneself outside oneself' that Bakhtin terms *exotropia*, not as 'another I', but in an objectual splitting not without emotional investment. Objects as signs or signs transformed into objects, which mark both an obsessive temporality and a displaced spatiality. Anticipating what would become a more clearly defined tendency in terms of the deployment of biographical space in the visual arts,[38] at the end of the seventies his work involved series, inventories and archives in a form of 'self-museumification', using photography and objects, which, in fact, defied temporality and ephemerality – and, hence, death: 'Art is a way to prevent death, the flight of time ... All the archival work I've done from the beginning, this wish to keep track of everything, certainly translates this kind of desire, a desire to halt death in its tracks.'[39] Thus one of his first works, made in 1969, was *Search for and Presentation of Everything Remaining from My Childhood 1944–50*, an artist's book containing an accumulation of perfectly banal objects of no particular provenance; a later piece, *Attempt at Reconstitution of Objects that Belonged to Christian Boltanski between 1948 and 1954*, was produced between 1970 and 1971. This objectuality – photographs, the remnants of a variety of materials, boxes, clothing, lights – with at times a sinister aura, was transformed in his characteristically expressive mode to address a range of themes, particularly those related to the traumatic memory of the Shoah, often in terrifying accumulations that indirectly and allegorically evoke those of the extermination camps. Indirectly and allegorically, because the aim of his installations is not to recreate an accurate representation of a scene, and the clothing does not consist of 'real objects' (as happens in some Holocaust museums) but is contemporary and arranged with the intention of being recognized as such, just as the photographs that make up certain memorial installations are not necessarily of the victims.

The clothes appeared in my work as an obvious development: I established a relationship between clothing, photography, and dead bodies. My work always says something about the relationship between collectives and individuals: each person is unique, but at the same time the number of them is staggering. Clothes are a way for me to represent many, many people. Like photographs. When I did my first piece in my studio, I honestly don't believe I had the clothes of the Shoah in mind. It's a completely obvious thing, but I don't think it occurred to me at first. It did come to me fairly quickly after that ...[40]

The relationship between the individual and the number, the idea of representing 'many people', makes his work a particularly unusual form of memorial experimentation with a strong imprint of the present.[41] From this comes the repeated attempt to pay tribute to names and faces – given the impossibility of giving an account of their lives, lives stalked by death: 'One thing that greatly interests me is the passage from the highly personal to the highly collective ... The artwork necessarily speaks about the self, but that's of no importance: it becomes each person.'[42] A work which problematizes artistic value, what might be called style:

My work poses questions about life, about our understanding of who we are, which are similar to questions a philosopher or a mystic asks. But instead of using words, I use images. With a work, you have its artistic value, which you could call style, and then you have the questions it asks. All my works are about asking questions.[43]

If the accumulation of objects piled in a space defines the style of his work, then the long journey taken by those works through different cities and countries (not only of Europe) and their successive transformations related to context, place (hangars, former synagogues, colleges, decommissioned factories, walls, train stations), not to mention well-known museums, biennials and galleries, is also part of that definition and the intended impact, which always has personal implications: 'The artist reveals to people looking at the work something that's already inside them, something they know deep down, and he brings it up to their consciousness.'[44] Place, here, acquires a special relevance in terms of geography, history, language, the traces of a past that the images may commemorate, and the space of the installation itself, laid out with reference to light, trajectories, the movement of bodies, their reaction to intentional obstacles, the physical sensation that accompanies the visual. It is a memorial journey that reaches out to those who remember, who follow old footsteps, who *return*, occasionally, over the traces of tragedy.[45]

It is worth mentioning here a curious existential coincidence between Boltanski and Sebald: they were both born in 1944, one in Paris, the other in Bavaria, and although neither of them had first-hand experience of the horrors of the war, its huge impact on their subjective construction is clearly manifest in their works. While the first year of Sebald's life was passed under menacing – although distant – skies filled with fighter planes, Boltanski was born not long after the liberation of France in a house with an attic where his Jewish father had lived in hiding, with the neighbours believing he was either absent or had been disappeared. And if the shadow of war never ceased to loom over the former, to the point of feeling he was a product of it, the latter (the child of an unusual mixed marriage: his mother was Christian, his father a Jewish convert to Christianity, both with vaguely left-wing sympathies) reveals a similar condition – sensation – in his autobiography:

> The war, the fact that I'm Jewish – these are the most important things to have happened to me in my life. And that's without having experienced the war, without really being Jewish: I was a child of the Shoah more than a child of Judaism, [it is] the main event that totally conditioned my life. I think it's such an exceptional event, so incomprehensible that once you know about it, you cannot go on the same way as before.[46]

Although biography occupies a very important space in the work of both authors, there are notable differences in the ways it is manifested. Sebald constructs a story of himself through autobiographical fiction and the essay – particularly in the works cited here – turning his gaze to the world rather than on himself – or speaking of himself through that gaze – in a form of writing whose power and originality come close to producing a new genre, one that is unclassifiable in terms of conventional parameters. Indeed, the repeated use

of indirect speech, the way in which real-life references and
fiction articulate with observations and personal reflections,
the subtle, seamless transitions from one to the other, from
a story – or biography – to another register in a reticulated
weave that at times screens the narrator himself, makes
the reading a journey simultaneously intimate and distant,
where autobiographical elements are translated as profound
experience rather than details of an event.

Boltanski, for his part, ironizes autobiography and memory
in his early works (see above) and then visually addresses
the concept of autofiction in the installation *10 Portraits
Photographiques de Christian Boltanski, 1946–1964*,[47] which
are in fact photographs of other children and young men, and
in *Les Saynètes Comiques*,[48] in which he intervenes in photographs of himself with paint and appears as father, mother
and son. This false self-referencing, which clearly expresses,
in the words of Régine Robin, 'the impossible narration of
oneself',[49] and the interchangeable trace of every biography,
forms the basis of work in which the collective – the shared
– predominates:

> [The idea (of *Inventories*) was] to gather together everything
> a person leaves behind to make an inverted portrait ... The
> *Inventories* say nothing about anyone. Their only interest is that
> anyone who looks at them sees his or her own portrait in them,
> since we all own pretty much the same objects: we all have a bed,
> a toothbrush, a comb ... We learn more about ourselves than the
> person behind the inventory.[50]

So, for example, *Album des photos de la Famille D.
1939–1964 [Photo Album of Family D, 1934–1964]*[51] (an
installation consisting of 150 photographs from the album of
a 'typical' family, which he enlarges and frames, composing
a wall that is randomly organized in terms of the theme and
temporality) occupies, as the artist himself says, the place
of his own album – 'I've never liked talking about myself
and I've always concealed my real life'[52] – and also, in the
sheltering silence of the letter *D*, of anyone's, of everyone's
album.[53] This indirect mode of approaching biographical
space is based on a particular conception of art: 'Art is more
interesting when it isn't directly autobiographical, even if the

artist's personality doesn't play an important role. I think
that one can, in a pinch, use oneself as a generic example, but
one's own story isn't communicable. It's only interesting if it
becomes collective.'[54]

His autobiography, *The Possible Life of Christian
Boltanski*, based on interviews with Catherine Grenier –
a text that retains a conversational structure, revisiting
the Socratic dialogue in the search of an explanation and
motivation; that is, some truth – establishes, step by step,
the relationship between life and works to the point that
each of them is firmly anchored in a personal circumstance.
That 'possible life', with its dazzling irony and autofiction,
plus an unexpected vein of humour, lingers on the intimacy
and everyday unfolding of childhood (and his parents'
traumatic story) only to then focus on the highs and lows of
a trajectory, its vicissitudes, fame, relationships with others.
Here objects, time and place are also insistently in evidence.
The family home, which was also the prison that saved his
father, is transformed into an environment he finds difficult to
leave behind, as is his obsession with objects due to temporality, due to what they retain after the death of their owners,
the emotional investment they represent, what they replace
and embody; in short, due to their virtual power as objects
of desire, *objet petit a*, in the Lacanian definition.

For a person who neither wanted to talk about his 'real
life' or accept a Proustian influence in his work – as has been
postulated by certain critics – but who tended to prioritize
great numbers, awaken collective identification and memory,
the development (also obsessive) of his 'possible' biography
– where the adjective and other scattered allusions signal
that it could be both true and false, is characteristic. As if
the absence of words that accompanies his works – which
are about absence – must be retrospectively compensated
for by a telling all, by a detailed and all-embracing map, a
chronology, anecdotes, opinions and sensations. It is indeed
a dialogic utterance, prompted by pertinent questions in strict
temporal and thematic order, one that could hardly have been
produced by the solitary exercise of writing. And it is also
true that, in this case, life sheds some light on the work and,
it might be said, offers an argument against those who accuse
that work of being a 'mannerism of suffering', something he

himself notes in a passage from his dialogue with Grenier. As with any autobiography, it is not just a matter of balance, of that giving form – and order – to life that only narrative makes possible, or of battling – with other weapons – against finitude: 'The work you and I are doing together in these interviews is also part of this wish to gather everything up before dying'[55]; there is also the issue of marking out future spaces of the voices, of what others might say afterwards, with the almost obligatory hindsight of biographies.

> My desire to survive, this desire we all have finds expression in ... the construction of an 'exemplary life'. I don't mean my private life, but the tales they'll tell about me. It sounds funny but it's true, and what we're doing with these interviews is constructing an exemplary life. It's a way of transmitting what doesn't get communicated through the object, but through stories. So since I don't write, a part of my exemplary life passes through the word, through anecdotes.[56]

The distinction between private and 'exemplary' life (the latter being what biography constructs) is interesting in that it signals exactly that notion of *example* which life necessarily assumes in narrative, whatever the intention of the protagonist.

Biographies/autobiographies

... the art of biography is the most restricted of all the arts
... The novelist is free; the biographer is tied.
Virginia Woolf (1974)

In the vague hope of leaving a trace, how does the idea of writing a biography arise? What is it that leads the biographer to retrace the steps of another, to investigate the details of a trajectory? Is it the fascination of the work, the search for the keys to a life, the mystery of an inner world? Is it the illusion of – the passion for – restoring a presence, for *doing justice*? In the thrilling pages of his *Works on Paper* and *Basil Street Blues*,[57] the English biographer Michael Holroyd offers some answers to that question of retrospective speech – an elusive temporality that is best expressed in the future perfect, what will have been. With humour, irony and a familiarity that is perhaps part of his chosen craft, in the various chapters of a voyage around places, times and people, he invites us to share the vicissitudes of his relationships with the illustrious lives masterfully depicted, according to critics, in his writing – Lytton Strachey, William Gherardie, Augustus John and George Bernard Shaw, among others: the entropic culmination of arduous, dogged research, in which the fundamental disorder of an existence, the intangible truth of another's experience, acquires a *form* – that the real life did not have – and, with that, a meaning, or rather an opening to multiple meanings.

The motivations are many and different: an interest in the intellectual world of England in the early twentieth century, that 'contemporary being', as Barthes would say, with names already enshrined in his childhood literary tastes, people who had been insufficiently recognized or unjustly forgotten. His modes of research vary according to the case, although they share a desire for thoroughness without which – one imagines – it is impossible to approach the innumerable defeats of a life. So, an obsessive, almost sleuth-like search leads him to immerse himself in manuscripts,[58] drafts, letters, documents, portraits, preserved objects, environments – the home, the study, the garden, the library[59] – to follow the same paths in order to *see* the same things, to interview a great number of people in order to gather their memories, to gain the confidence of executors and circumvent testamentary arguments. A colossal endeavour in which, according to the author, the figure of the archaeologist appears, hoping to throw light on remnants and fragments (in relation to the life of the writer, for instance, it is a sometimes unexpected part of the text of his work), a figure who must advance along the fine line between personal involvement and historical perspective, between fact and emotion.

In contrast to a work of fiction, which has no responsibility to attend to facts and whose author does not need to identify with the characters, biographical genres, as Bakhtin[60] pointed out, involve a splitting of the self that in some way sets biographers and autobiographers on an equal footing: in order to construct their characters, the former must immerse themselves in the lives of others; on objectifying their own stories, the latter stand outside themselves to see themselves through *the eyes of others*. The frontier between biography and autobiography is not, therefore, so clearly defined, and in fact, as Holroyd observes, there is a great deal of the autobiographical in the mode of approaching that life of the other and also an ethical limit: not confusing oneself with that other. This subtle imbrication makes it interesting to observe how – from that *other side*, from the narration of the experience (and its vicissitudes) of the person who intends to trace out the distinctive features of a life (the subject of the biography) – the figure of the biographer develops almost unconsciously in the background. Perhaps one of the most original ideas in Holroyd's texts is the felicitous inter-action achieved between literary writing, research guide and theoretical thought.

The idea of rescuing 'personages insufficiently recognized or unjustly forgotten' by means of biographies constituted on genre models – as is the case of Lytton Strachey, Augustus John and Patrick Hamilton, for example – is not only relevant at an ethical level – doing justice to a trajectory – or in terms of what it can add to knowledge and the re-evaluation of a body of scientific, literary or artistic work in the context of a particular era; it is also important as a critical positioning with respect to the reigning value parameters of a cultural sphere. This positioning is characteristic of Holroyd's work and is extended to a vast constellation of British authors whose works have been, in his opinion, unfairly overlooked.[61]

From the appearance in the mid-seventeenth century of John Aubrey's[62] *Brief Lives*,[63] which formed a landmark in the English biographical tradition through its portrayal of the essence of a person in a few pages – sometimes a single paragraph – to the unwieldy reconstructions that populate the global heritage, the genre has passed through many stages and in recent decades has experienced a new golden age. According to Holroyd, it has been seen as 'the poor relation of history'[64] or used to fix identity in eras of uncertain authority, but it has changed with the times and, in his opinion, will continue to change: it will become more personal, more imaginative, experimental, hybrid, moving progressively further from the 'lives and letters' conception of the genre; there will be fewer unitary stories covering life and death, and more selective stories, a year, an event, a work, a particular story.[65] Artistic freedom to create and confidence in the authenticated event: this is a desirable formula for the author.

While a biography is normally constructed around the figure of a notable life, accentuating the features that make it singular, any attempt in that respect cannot fail to demonstrate that it is always a life lived with others and also *for* others. And in this sense, as with the story of any life, it tends to produce identification – either related to glamour or trauma – or, as occurs with Holroyd himself, to generate 'an intimacy between strangers'.[66] It is no coincidence that this expression appears in a textual encounter, 'With Virginia Woolf at Sheffield Place', a chapter of Holroyd's autobiography that can be read as a tribute to Woolf, who detested the boring parade of dates, battles and notes of conventional forms of biography and wanted to revolutionize the genre, make it accessible to ordinary readers, 'clear those forests of family trees planted from father to son in the colonising territory of male culture'.[67] Later he confesses:

> This is what attracted me to biography: the idea of an 'intimacy between strangers'; a closeness growing up during the acts of writing and reading between an author, the reader and their subject, all unknown to one another before the book began coming into existence. For I do not think of biography as being an information-retrieval exercise: information, now the fruit of technology, has little fascination for me unless it takes root in my emotions and grows in my imagination into knowledge. What increasingly absorbs me is the unconscious process of learning. While writing I forget myself, and when I return to my world I sense that I am someone slightly different.[68]

Intimacy, closeness, an emotional community between the participants, the creation of bonds of complicity. True, those signifiers could also be attributed to fiction and to what its authors imagine their relationship with readers to be. But here, in the genres discussed, there is something extra that Bakhtin called *biographical value*: that thing which, in every story, every attempt to give – verbal or audiovisual – form to a life questions both the narrator and the narratee with respect to their own existence in terms of ethics, aesthetics and, we might even say, politics. That ephemeral communion, that virtual tuning-in, is what surely feeds the constant desire to glimpse 'real lives' while being aware of how vain that desire is, how intangible that reality, how inevitably fictional the whole story.

If, as readers of biographies and autobiographies, we feel the urge to participate in that 'intimacy between strangers' which generates the story – as if someone were personally, face to face, telling us about their life – the preceding process of accompanying the biographer on her/his quest involves a further step; a form of vote of confidence that includes us in the exploration (where the secret feeds creation) and the act of giving value to objects and places, the difficulty of crossing the threshold of intimacy, the limit of discretion (which, according to the biographer Lytton Strachey, is not the best part of a biography), the hesitations, the digressions, the unexpected findings. Like that moment when, following the trail of the painter Augustus John, the author of an important but unjustly neglected body of work, Holroyd discovers another figure in the weave, that of his sister, Gwen John, an artist in exile (in Paris), Rodin's lover, a person ahead of her time whose work dazzles him as strongly as her life.[69] In this case, the biography appears to be the demonstration of an unforeseen, everyday truth: life inseparable from other lives, an endless *mise en abîme*. In the construction of the person, the guile of avoiding weaknesses, sordid sides, unspeakable aspects also come into play. Here Holroyd, when reflecting on the long English tradition of biography, tells us that, even taking into account factual rigour and necessary ethical concerns, the outcome is to some extent always subjective.

In terms of emotion, imagination and knowledge, that subjectivity accounts for the particular relationship he establishes with his biographees: a distance that allows them to 'be known' without an overload of interpretation through their letters and works, scenes retrieved from testimony, and a simultaneous familiar closeness, like someone who participated in those scenes, as an amiable onlooker, through ironic, humour-filled, critical moments, with an attitude that, rather than indulgent, is considerate and evaluative. This quotation from Lytton Strachey perhaps expresses it well: 'Human beings are too important to be treated as mere symptoms of the past ... They have a value which is independent of any temporal process – which is eternal, and must be felt for its own sake.'[70]

That value is also expressed in the way Holroyd analyses the works of the subjects of his biographies, positioning them in a social context that extends beyond themselves.

> Patrick Hamilton is an expert guide to English social distinctions, with all their snobbish mimicry and fortified non-communication. He describes wonderfully well how the hyphenated upper classes, yelling at their dogs, splashing in their baths like captured seals, and writing their aloof letters in the third person (like broadcasters recounting an athletic event), remain so mysterious to the lower breeds. Taking us out of the pub into the swarming streets of London, he gives us a social map of this malignant city as it was in the harsh commercial era of the 1920s and the early 1930s. His Marxism became a method of distinguishing between the avoidable and the unavoidable suffering of people, and, insofar as literature can change social conditions, such a vivid facsimile in fiction may have helped us to do so.[71]

How does a well-known biographer write his autobiography, expanding on the features he allows readers to glimpse when narrating the lives of others? In 'Two Types of Ambiguity' in *Basil Street Blues* he tells us:

> ... after my father and mother died in the nineteen-eighties I began to feel a need to fill the space they left with a story. Neither of them was on the front line of great historical events: their dramas are the dramas of ordinary lives, each one nevertheless extraordinary. From their accounts, from various photograph albums and a few clues in two or three boxes of miscellaneous odds and ends, I want to recreate the events that would give my own fragmented upbringing a context. Can I stir those few remnants and start a flame, an illumination? This book is not simply a search for facts, but for echoes and associations, signs and images, the recovery of a lost narrative and a sense of continuity: things I seem to miss and believe I never had.[72]

In this short paragraph, I find a number of the key features of the genre in its innumerable contemporary variants: the idea that every life deserves to be told[73]; the identification that produces what is shared in every story; the place of photography and objects in the exercise of memory, which can be seen in the work of all the authors mentioned here; illumination as a metaphor for what is discovered, and the configurative role of narration – its biographical value – that is capable of going beyond the facts to articulate and give continuity to the innumerable traces, 'echoes and associations, signs and images'[74] that, in a disordered fashion, inhabit every human being.

Returning to the lives of others, although the singular individual is still at centre stage, the frontiers of biography, Holroyd tells us, have expanded to the point where 'its subject matter is pretty well now the whole range of human experience, insofar as it can be recovered'.[75] This is a statement that once again – and not by chance – brings up the concept of the loss of human experience that Benjamin develops in his famous essay *The Storyteller*.[76] There, the philosopher casts a critical eye over the radical transformation that modern technology introduced into narrative habits (at one extreme, the gaps in the communicable that the destructive experience of the First World War brought with it but also the emphasis on the individual in the novel, silent reading, the distance of the communications media) and the ensuing end of old stories, told orally by the storyteller to the community, with their tendency to be re-elaborated and reinterpreted as authentic sources of experience, and of the exchange of experiences. This is not by chance, as was said, because Holroyd concludes the chapter 'What Justifies Biography' with the following: 'By recreating the past we are calling on the same magic as our forebears did with the stories of their ancestors round the fires under night skies. The need to do this, to keep death in its place, lies deep in human nature, and the art of biography arises from that need. This is its justification.'[77]

It may be, then, that in the turbulent contemporary world, in the dogged customs of biographers, that loss finds the possibility of restitution. The storyteller: 'his distinction is to be able to tell his *entire life*. The Storyteller: he is the man who could let the wick of his life be completely consumed by the gentle flame of his story'[78] (my italics).

Recapitulations

Why the choice of those three voices to offer answers to the questions posed at the beginning of this chapter? (Or perhaps the question is simply: why do we make choices?) A direct, assertive response might be: their relevance to the topic. But there is always something else behind academic rationales, something we may be only partially aware of that makes us privilege one option over other, equally acceptable ones. In this case, the questions came afterwards, inspired by the way in which, in my reading, dissimilar works could be brought into dialogue, each appreciated according to its own style and, in turn, the indirect or allegorical mode, the digression that each of them posits in order to approach their sensitive, delicate material: biography, memory, pivotal themes in my own work. Digression as method, to the extent, as Benjamin suggests, that it involves 'the renunciation of the uninterrupted progress of an intention';[79] that is to say, it critiques the conception of method as a continuous path which can be replicated in any situation. A method, then, which suggests recognition of the fracturing of temporality, the persistence of the object in its different gradations of meaning, the fragmentary emergence and the juxtaposition of heterogeneous elements, aspects that these three creative practitioners display in their different modes.

Digression is also a distancing from the fact and the endeavour to speak of it 'as it is', an explicit recognition of the symbolic dimension, the impossibility of bringing back scenes and moments; the assumption that we only have stories of stories and that the *form* the story takes is essential. This is a distance that all three establish in relation to their own biographies: what is allowed to be seen, what is translated, and what unexpectedly emerges in reading. That indirect mode of speaking of oneself in the work, whether it be in a fictional plot (Sebald), the accumulation of objects (Boltanski) or by allowing a glimpse of oneself behind the biographies of others (Holroyd), is, once again, proof of the multifaceted nature of contemporary biographical space, where revitalized canonical genres coexist with a wide variety of other forms in a process of growing hybridization. So, perhaps in confirmation of certain predictions in literature and the arts, academic research, the communications and social media, existential narratives of every variety have accepted the challenge of finding new ways to approach an ever more elusive *I* (we).[80] And one might also consider the closer inclusion in the dialogue, in a different vein, of the familiar *you* consistently used by advertising, interactive media, self-help works, bio/political rhetoric, the therapeutic state and the 'worthy causes' of the global environment.

In that intersubjective circuit, in that 'intimacy between strangers' created by biographical genres, the artist and authors considered here trace their own figures. Boltanski and Holroyd give way to the temptation of autobiography beyond what the retrospective work can say of them: personal concerns, value judgements, styles, influences. The need to tell – or the passion for telling – a story leads them to that 'recovery of experience' which involves returning over the trodden path, recomposing scenes and memories, bringing together the strands of the progression of lost days. Boltanski does this in what might be called 'life as conversation' – and then in some way rescuing Benjamin's lost orality; Holroyd, in a subtle literary weave that also emphasizes the interpersonal warmth of the narrative. Both of them allow us a glimpse of childhood memories, family life, the beginnings of a vocation and the creative challenges of their works without concealing references to 'life' in general, as is also expected of autobiography. For his part, Sebald (in the gravity of his prose, in that indefatigable march that appears like the chronotope[81] par excellence of his writing – *The Rings* ...*Vertigo* ... *The Emigrants*, *Austerlitz* – in the storyteller-like character he constructs. '"When someone goes on a trip, he has a story to tell" goes the German saying, and people imagine the storyteller as someone who has come from afar'[82]) scatters only scraps of information along the path, but there too a depth of experience is framed, far from everyday trifles, in the world unfolding before our eyes. A chance, perennial panorama, a landscape of the slow destruction of nature, of human catastrophes and the decay of things and beings and also of imaginary worlds, where the influence of Borges is perfectly clear. The gaze as autobiography, it could be said.

I was also interested in the tension between singularity and number, between the individual values that reaffirm an auto/biography – in Simmel's[83] sense, as human qualities with a degree of independence from the social – and those things capable of addressing what is shared: in Sebald, as the evocation of exceptional people in counterpoint to the annihilating effects of catastrophe; in Boltanski, as objectual reiteration of the presence of the one among the all; in Holroyd, as the individual value given to an experience that can indeed be shared. The number of horror also stalks the works of Boltanski and Sebald, linked to traumatic remembrance: in Sebald, it is present in the crushing details of aerial bombardments and their victims, the devastating effects of a hurricane on a forest and the constantly repeated historical massacres; in Boltanski, it is the insistent visual agglomeration of objects, an excess of presence that connotes only absence.[84]

The fascinating relationship between word and image – its reciprocity – was also involved in my selection. The image as the triumph of metaphor in the work of Sebald, in subtle dialogue with the black-and-white photographs that appear from time to time on the pages, often with a ghostly air, not to illustrate what is being narrated but to introduce a perturbing inflection, and objectual and temporal distancing; the photograph in the work of Boltanski, with its mournful or vaguely sinister weight, in solidarity or articulation with other elements; the place of the photograph, the family album; the portraits, in the biographical creation of a character – and himself – in Holroyd.

Digression, distance, is also a mode of addressing the incisive issue of representation – and possibly all knowledge. The *how* of speaking and showing, of narrating a life or an event, of bringing the happy or traumatic memory – remembrance – to the present and the intrinsic difficulty involved in the latter. Sebald expresses this unequivocally in his concern for how to represent the war scenes in certain stories without prejudice to the epiphanies that can, with all validity, be found in literature in relation to such scenes:

> But it is one thing for the words really to take off, another for them to be tastelessly overloaded, as in this much-cited passage, with recherché adjectives, nuances of literary colour, a tinselly

glitter, and other cheap ornaments. When a morally compromised author claims the field of aesthetics as a value-free area it should make his readers stop and think.[85]

That taking-off of words as if unaided, without being overloaded, could be the best description of his own style, where economy and metaphorical density are united in a uniquely poetic prose. While his themes differ, Holroyd is also concerned with the indissoluble relationship between ethics and aesthetics, which is expressed in his work in the obligatory principle of veridiction of the biography and in *delicacy*, a figure that I suggest he privileges in his exploration of private worlds, without explicitly defining it as such. A figure that also refers to Barthes, who, very much in the mode of Holroyd, relates it to small details, consideration, courtesy and even levity: Plato, he reminds us in *A Lover's Discourse*,[86] speaks of the *delicacy/tact*[87] of the goddess Ate, whose 'foot is winged' and 'touches lightly'.[88]

Boltanski, for his part, as does Sebald, confronts the difficulty of interrogating the traumatic memory of violence and horror but this time from the visual sphere and, like Sebald, understands that such an endeavour necessitates both ethical involvement and an aesthetic challenge, the possibility of saying and the threshold of what cannot be communicated, the potential of the word and the image and also a recognition of their limitations, what no effort of the memory can ever recover. Based on that conviction, he develops a style in which the accumulation of elements is significant, the raw image of facts is absent, and it is objects that condense the evocative power, recounting the tragedy and the *number* as an atrocious signifier. It could even be thought that the painful litany of figures in Sebald's *Natural History*, the constant bombardments, the tons of bombs, miles of dead – and his enumeration *sans frontières* of the sites of concentration camps – find a precise, austere correlation in Boltanski's installations, one which is capable of articulating the descriptive and metaphorical potential of the story with a possible – or impossible – image on which the eyes rest.

I've never directly shown an image of violence in what I do [Boltanski tells Grenier]. I don't think one can do that. As a rule,

people who show violence do so to denounce it. But looking at
those images is never harmless and there's a side of us that enjoys
looking at suffering. It's true for me, at any rate. And I think it's
the case for everyone.[89]

However, as the artist himself admits, the question is not
settled: and that is exactly where the dilemma of the image is
located, in its *seeing or not seeing*. So a little later he returns
to the topic in the conversation, this time in relation to a bitter
controversy that was raging in France at that time about an
exhibition[90] in which four photographs from the Archives
of the Auschwitz-Birkenau State Museum were exhibited,
accompanied by a narrative.[91] One cannot talk about the
camps, Boltanski says, because it's an unknown experience;
they can't even be photographed, 'but in reality, I don't
know if those photographs should be shown or not ... except
maybe in the context of a historical museum; in any case
they shouldn't be shown in an art exhibit.' Nevertheless, he
later accepts that, as the Shoah is 'such a strange, exceptional
event', one has to go on speaking of it in order to 'understand
it, mourn it and try to ensure that it never happens again'.[92]
Despite the swings in this argument – as often occurs in any
discussion on the topic – the artist appears to have found
his place in that elusive, allegorical visuality, in those images
that set off on their own path, remotely, but which, however,
evoke a historicity and a commitment, a positioning. In
terms of reception, the problem may arise from a change
of scale – as happens with *Personne* – when the exhibit
becomes spectacle and loses the intimacy of place, the close
relationship between the body and the surrounding space.
This is an issue frequently raised in contemporary art, where
monumentality, particularly in large international exhibitions, conspires, according to its critics, against meaning.

Taking different routes, each of the creative practitioners
in this dialogic exchange has brought with him a number
of responses to those questions posed at the beginning of
the chapter, and has added new ones. They have allowed
a glimpse of the subtle articulation between biography and
memory, the passion within the writing of a life, the places –
physical and symbolic – that make up a biography, including
our own, the difficulty of dealing with traumatic memory

– which speaks to us very intimately here in Argentina – and the dilemmas of representation that, although attentive to the communion between ethics and aesthetics, to a reflexive and metaphorical *making visible*, leave open the field of what cannot be expressed. And finally, each of them has also managed, through their work, to vindicate – returning to Benjamin – the unbreakable bond between narrative and justice.

3

Memory and Image

... the extreme violence of cruelty hovers at the edge of the image, of all images.[1]

Jean-Luc Nancy (2005)

I would like to begin with an image that is not an image, or rather that is a literary image, framed in the endless profundity of the word, in its poetics. It is a fragment from *Austerlitz*,[2] a novel by the German writer and academic W. G. Sebald that has received great public and critical acclaim. The novel – which the author himself prefers to call a book of prose of indefinable genre – is a long story in which the narrator, having met a stranger, one Jacques Austerlitz, in the waiting room of the train station in Antwerp, recounts, without stopping for breath – by which I mean, in a single paragraph – the decades-long conversation they continued, during various encounters, most of them casual, in other stations and cities. A fascinating conversation, almost a monologue, in which Austerlitz, a solitary, melancholy person, inseparable from his rucksack, relates – and so brings to light – snippets of his life, a life with a mystery that resists the search for identity that takes him on a constant journey – like the 'without stopping for breath' of the narrative – from one place to another. Taken in at an early age by a Welsh preacher and his wife from a remote mountain village, his identity was a secret carried to the grave by his reserved adoptive parents, who only left him one disturbing clue: the name he bore was not his true name.

On that urgent, hopeless quest, in the middle of the book, Austerlitz – the narrator tells us – finally discovers the key to the mystery. During his relentless journey around different European railway stations and cities, he has always felt a strange attraction, replete with a confusion of sensations, for London's Liverpool Street, to which he frequently returns. One day, following someone going towards a disused area of the station, he discovers a former ladies' waiting room. He goes in and is rooted to the spot by a flood of images and memories:

> In fact I felt, said Austerlitz, that the waiting room where I stood as if dazzled contained all the hours of my past life, all the suppressed and extinguished fears and wishes I had ever entertained, as if the black and white diamond pattern of the stone slabs beneath my feet were the board on which the end-game would be played, and it covered the entire plane of time. Perhaps that is why, in the gloomy light of the waiting room, *I also saw* two middle-aged people dressed in the style of the thirties [he describes them]. And I not only *saw* the minister and his wife, said Austerlitz, *I also saw* the boy they had come to meet. He was sitting by himself on a bench over to one side. His legs, in white knee-length socks, did not reach the floor, and but for the small rucksack he was holding on his lap I don't think I would have known him, said Austerlitz. As it was, I recognized him by that rucksack of his[3] (my italics).

At that moment he understood, as far as the shred of involuntary memory allowed, that he must have arrived there, in that station, over half a century before, one of so many other Jewish children – as is later revealed – sent by their parents from an area gradually being overtaken by Nazism in the hope that, as refugees, they would be saved from the imminent tragedy.[4]

The text continues:

> All I do know is that when *I saw* the boy sitting on the bench I became aware, through my dull bemusement, of the destructive effect on me of my desolation through all those past years, and

a terrible weariness overcame me at the idea that I had never
really been alive, or was only now being born, almost on the eve
of my death.[5]

That 'saw' continues over the following pages among
the nightmarish fog and the series of mental disturbances
produced by the revelation, leading him to whisper: 'I merely
saw myself waiting on a quay in a long crocodile of children
lined up two by two, most of them carrying rucksacks or
small leather cases ... *I saw* ... the bows of the ship, higher
than a house, the seagulls fluttering over our heads and
screeching wildly... .'[6]

Once he has discovered his identity, Austerlitz's wanderings
inevitably take him to Prague, where he rediscovers his
former family home and, in it, the woman who cared for
him as a child. This enables him to begin to fill the gaps in
his story: his mother had died in the Terezin concentration
camp – the next stage of his journey – and the last trace of his
father had been in Paris, where he also goes in search of him.

As the woman shows him a photograph in which he
himself appears dressed in a strange outfit and long white
socks, about to accompany his mother to a masked ball, she
tells him:

> One has the impression, she said, of something stirring in them,
> as if one caught small sighs of despair, *gémissements de désespoir*
> was her expression, said Austerlitz, as if the pictures had a
> memory of their own and remembered us, remembered the role
> that we, the survivors, and those no longer among us had played
> in our former lives. Yes, and the small boy in the other photo-
> graph, said Věra after a while, this is you Jacquot, in February
> 1939, about six months before you left Prague ... The picture lay
> before me, said Austerlitz, but I dared not touch it.[7]

Why have I begun in this way, with such a long introduction?

First, because this was the recollection that emerged as
soon as I began to think about the relationship between
memory and image, and then the possible politics of the
transmission of memory. An image from somewhere that
wasn't the usual visual bombardment – and its violence –
or the questions raised by public memory and theoretical
reflection. However, as often happens with literature, that

heart-rending image of the boy of four and a half – as we later learn – whose feet don't reach the ground, who appears quietly in a slight inflection of the writing, contains not only the key to the story and the discovery of identity – an image that awakens memory, a memory that awakens the image – but also key concepts in this area of critical thought. The intrinsic relationship between memory and image, for example; the emotional weight and the bodily impact that supposes; its *eventfulness*, in terms of the transformation of the state of things and the essential role of temporality, the paradoxical tension between presence and absence; the irreducible nature of personal experience that is always collective. There, *we see* – as Austerlitz repeatedly *saw* – a whole era appearing in the depth of the word, in the image of the boat, the quay, the screeching seagulls, the sound and fury – to following a literary vein. A *seeing* that in Sebald is complemented by the strange black-and-white photographs that symptomatically accompany his texts.

But why *see* that *depth of the word*? Simply for its ironic dimension, that prodigious ability of language, of the sign, to unite an acoustic image, as Saussure defines it, with a concept that is potentially also an image. This is a first indication that the two orders considered here – the verbal and the visual – are not to be separated, are intrinsically bound, although clearly not *the same*.

The ancient Greeks reflected long and hard on the dazzling relationship between memory and image, its potential for illuminating dormant, crouching, negated, repressed areas, and they even gave thought to the performative iconicity of language in terms of its almost pictorial capacity for *creation* and *imagination*. The philosopher Paul Ricoeur returns to the topic in his penultimate great work,[8] focusing on the transit between memory and history essential to any transmission. For Aristotle, for example, a memory is an image and carries with it, from its own etymology, fantasy and the imagination; for Plato, memory is an imprint, like a footmark in wax – or even an affliction of the soul – that, as with a graphic print, can be translated into writing.

So what is it that memory attempts to conceal from forgetting? What is it that it wants to transmit, to leave as an indelible mark on the collective memory? The events of the past, one might say, although in the case of its evils, its 'misfortunes', with their tally of violence, suffering and fear, a certain tempering comes into play so that they are unrepeatable but not *unbearable* in shared life.[9] However, it is no easy task to respond to the 'what' of memory. There is 'something' that is remembered – a mark on the cerebral cortex – and, more importantly, an emotional mark that, as was seen in the story at the beginning of this chapter, remains as its originating imprint. So, according to Aristotle, on calling something to mind, one remembers an image, a 'picture' whose intrinsic relationship to the imagination goes hand in hand with the problem of representation (and, therefore, its weak relationship to truth) plus the emotion that the image carries with it. Which, then, does the memory carry most strongly: the image of the absent thing or the present emotion? And is the arrival of that image in memory involuntary or is it due to the work of remembrance?[10]

In *Austerlitz*, there is an active search for the past through clues and a revelation (a remembrance?) that anticipates the memory of loss, showing the complete oblivion of the traumatic scene, which lies like an unconscious trace, a classic survival mechanism. But there is also a sense of disquiet, a presumption of something that is always lacking, a secret mark that drives the work of discovery and that leads – as in the case of the illegally appropriated children assigned by the repressors to other parents during the last Argentinian military dictatorship – to a desire to know more, to confront the fear of knowing, an obligatory complement to the anguish of not knowing.

That sudden revelation imposed on Austerlitz, that 'picture', to use an Aristotelian expression, that returns violently to the memory – the violence of enlightenment – as it shows itself, refers to something else: the absence that presence unfailingly carries in its wake. An absence that any appearance, any exercise of memory entails.

That is perhaps why every image, as Jean-Luc Nancy[11] perceives it, has a *ground*, something that escapes us, not only due to the absence of what is not there – the out-of-frame that forms an enigma or is always lacking in what appears – but also the disturbing shadow that temporality casts on it, reminding us of our mortality: the portrait, the photograph, the painting, the image recorded on the retina all testify to it. So, in the first excerpt quoted here, the irruption of memory carries with it the dazzling certainty of death.

The temporality of the image as loss, the subtle slippage of time – from which comes the strong emotional impact of photography – and also images *of time*, as in the use of variable light in painting, photography and cinema. And there may be a nuance here that could be added to Ricoeur's narrative theory in terms of his claim that temporality – in contrast to 'time' in the singular – can only be apprehended in narrative: the image also testifies to temporality and so is also narrative.

In this way, image and narration are inseparably united in every attempt – and so in all politics – to transmit memory. And this is as true for the iconic dimension of the word (which makes every story a projection screen of the imagination – imagination that is no less 'true' than what the images attest to) as for the narrative nature of the image, although this requires at least proximity to the word. In both cases, the idea of transmission carries a sense of intention, a tension between self and other (the addressee) that involves the dialogic movement of discourse – in its widest sense – and so *responds*, gives an answer and has *responsibility*.[12]

If that response is by definition ethical – according to a regime of truth, a value system that rules every discursive genre – in the case of the transmission of memory, it becomes an imperative, a duty in terms of justice, particularly with reference to murder, persecution and traumatic events that leave memories which cannot be silenced, whose temporality is always the present. Justice, as an ideal of truth beyond judicial power – although it can be appealed to – has a duty towards the victims, the events of the past and also towards the future, perceived as a potential improvement.

So, this being said, the full complexity of the topic becomes visible. What is transmitted? Who transmits it? How and why? Is the transmission of memory possible if, as claimed by Maurice Halbwachs (who postulated the term 'collective memory' a few years before his death in the Buchenwald concentration camp),[13] only individuals remember, if each person carries his or her own mark as a non-transferable experience? Is it, moreover, possible to speak of 'memory' when, despite the effort to find a universal signifier, the plurality of memories exceeds any hypothetical limit of consensus, not only as difference but also as conflict?

However, since one never remembers alone, as Halbwachs also notes, but rather in the context of a social environment, that transmission is the key and the 'gift' which guides the future of generations, the principle of recognition and belonging, the duty of History as a discipline and of the state as the guarantor of the institutions: multiple spaces for the unfolding of memories, from government to family levels, private and public, from the group to what can, if somewhat vaguely, be seen as the *collective*. Which is also to say multiple competing narratives that confront not only 'content' but also conceptions of representation, modes of enunciation, ethical and aesthetic positions; in short, forms of the story that are unequivocally involved in their construction of meaning.

In this construction, nothing is irrelevant: state policies on the ideal of justice (such as the ones that enable those accused of crimes against humanity to be tried) are of equal importance to the establishment of public places of memory (museums, monuments, memorials) or educational policies that include the recent past as an object of study and analysis. This being said, the range of questions opens out again in terms of forms, conceptions, styles, the risk of crystallization and aestheticization. To give just one example: a monument, as a landmark that will soon be lost in its surroundings, is not enough in itself; it is necessary to think of active, perceptive, enquiring modes of relating to materiality, in the way the reactive aesthetic of anti-monumentalism operates, laying greater emphasis on emptiness and absence, the fissure that trauma leaves in a society, than on the compensatory abundance of a finished, tranquillizing form.[14] But minimal, singular, commonplace memorials are also necessary, those that provoke questions between parents and children, teachers and students, that open spaces for debate, curiosity, disquiet in the face of what was not personally experienced. Debate and disquiet, or disquiet debate, is perhaps the best mode of construction – and transmission – of memory, which, of course, forgetting never totally eclipses.

Between the record of public, institutional, governmental and media memory, where testimony and the document are the prime administrators of the transition between memory and history, and everyday conversation, which also tends to produce meanings and practices (the 'practical reason' that, according to Bourdieu[15] directs the actions of individuals) there is another space of elaboration and transmission that, in my opinion, is privileged: that of art in all its manifestations.

The literature chosen to open this dialogue, while lacking the rigour expected of testimony – a necessary but impossible limiting to the strict truth of events; the harsh accumulation of detail that at times almost crosses the threshold of shame – is capable of achieving all the depth – and rawness – of a 'personal' experience and so is perhaps closer to the collective. *Austerlitz*, as a case in point, is an admirable exercise in the transmission of memory that, in turn, constructs the emblematic scene of that transmission: the story a person makes of his/her life in terms of a search for a lost memory, configuring it performatively as such in intelligible unity, for the other, the storyteller's singular 'you': a story that the narrator in turn tells us, establishing us as the 'you' of the present of the utterance. That unusual enunciative form allows us to tune into the *narration*, in the sense Benjamin gives it in 'The Storyteller',[16] as the exchange of stories and experiences in the context of shared listening, the opposite of the novel with its focus on the individual, the product of technology, and based on a life plan. The clear Benjaminian influence in Sebald's work and his own refusal to consider *Austerlitz* as a novel – the *novelesque*, in his opinion, is beset by melodrama – give authority, I believe, to that interpretation: the double distance of the traumatic event that allows both a tempering of its violence and its memory; an oblique, reported, indirect approach – again, digression – just as Sebald himself understood the theme of the 'final solution' could be addressed in writing; the double temporality of memory, simultaneously present and past, possibly another of its paradoxes.

The visual arts also face the challenge of distance and the dilemmas of representation (to which can be added the mystery of the 'unrepresentable'), plus the temptation to literalness or the drift of metaphor. The violence of the art of this time – or all times – that occasionally seems to vie with the violence of the image that assaults us in daily life, the violence of the event as it is and its eternal (re)production in graphic formats and on the screen. The violence of the image and the violent image, between the 'monstrance' and the monster,[17] although the violence of art – in contrast to violence per se – is distinguished by its lack of ground, that is to say, the place where the real is involved, where it opens itself to multiplicity of perception and interpretation.[18]

If I began with images from literature, I would like to end, so as to do justice to them as well, with certain art images that closely address memory and whose relevance to the epigraph of this section was suddenly revealed to me – but possibly not completely by chance – during a visit to the Musée d'art Moderne de la Ville de Paris a short time after reading *Austerlitz*. The exhibition was Christian Boltanski's *Storage Area of the Children's Museum*,[19] a 1989 installation donated to the museum, occupying two adjoining salons.

As was mentioned in the preceding chapter, for this artist, born in 1944, the same year as Sebald, the traumatic memory of Nazism and the Second World War is an equally strong inspiration in his work, which addresses the collective from a narrative aesthetic in which allusion and metaphor have primacy over direct representation. His work is characterized by the accumulation of everyday elements with no particular connotations but which in combination, as was seen, are deeply disturbing: clothes, with their immediate relationship to the category of *person*; display cases; faded photographs; many lit lamps in accordance with a Jewish tradition of paying tribute to the dead; wooden or cardboard figures casually garbed in clothing; a system of symbols in which the passage of time, the stalking presence of death, everyday sinister elements and the traumatic memory of the Shoah are stressed in a variety of ways. This obsessive *objecthood* often deals with infancy: his own, in the works mentioned above; that of other children, whose tragic fates can be guessed at from the treatment of the photographs (enlarged to the point of dissolution, out of focus, with deep shadows and lights shining on the faces that blur some of the features) or from the piles of clothing without any of the elements being related to 'real' people or objects. In other words, the photographs are not actual testimony of authentic victims and the clothing does not come from any depository of horrors. In this respect, as a detail important to an understanding of his work, the

artist once explained that his installations used clothing
that was easily identifiable as being contemporary, far from
having any historical pretensions or, of course, immediacy
with what is indirectly and metaphorically implied.

The impact of entering the salons of *Storage Area of
the Children's Museum* is immediate: the walls are lined
with metal shelving units filled with children's clothing, the
accumulation of which is quite simply terrifying. Here and
there, an individual item hangs down, becomes detached
from the pile and offers itself to the gaze on the edge of the
shelf – of the void – as a recognizable form. In one corner –
with an immediate connection to the scene from *Austerlitz*
mentioned above – is a form similar to a long, white sock.
At the far end of the room, a mural of blurred photographs
of children's faces is displayed without words, as a sort of
phantasmal memorial.

If, as Borges said, the aesthetic act consists of the imminence
of a revelation that never occurs, Boltanski's installation
completely fulfils that definition. It sinks one into a deep
place where personal memories mingle with images that (in)
form the collective store, what might tentatively be called
historical memory.

Curiously enough, the installation unfolded before me
without 'revealing' anything of the temporal arc of that
unfinished story of children who had escaped the horrendous
fate that had overcome others. And yet both scenes, the
literary and the visual, in the absence of any detail, displayed
the unequivocal edge of cruelty.

In this way there is a confluence of the two stations of
this brief journey, where art, language, memory and image
have woven a capricious, possibly arbitrary, fabric within the
orders of poetry and theory. A fabric that is possibly a means
of proposing other strands of reflection and transmission on
which methodological rigour does not have primacy over
openness, ethics and aesthetics, other dimensions of emotion
and experience.

4

Women Who Narrate: Autobiography and Traumatic Memories[1]

When fear, poverty or plague spread,
story telling falters on those points where order breaks down,
and then chronicles of invasions and defeats appear,
dark episodes with hidden wild beasts and the occasional king
and one is a fugitive under the skin,
as if inhabiting an intrusive paragraph in a black legend.

Olga Orozco (1998)[2]

The focus of this chapter is an analysis of the way in which biography (particularly autobiography), memory and testimony articulate in certain narratives from the recent past. In this case, the narratives of women recounting the traumatic experiences they suffered under the last Argentinian military dictatorship (1976–1983), beyond the legal declarations they made as witnesses in the trials of their repressors. Beyond, in a double temporality: chronology – twenty years later – and writing, whose mark not only exceeds the moment of inscription but also unfolds in anticipation of each reading. That writing is the focus of my attention: not so much in accounts of the 'events' as in modes of enunciation, the work of language that imposes on the experience – not merely representing it – the avatars of discourse in terms of the tropological figures of narration. This analytical stance does not involve any devaluation of what has been said (its value as evidence, once again) in the crimes against humanity committed (kidnapping, torture, imprisonment, murder, disappearance), its undeniable and necessary ethical dimension. And neither can the emotional impact, the shock that this type of account generates be set aside. What I attempt is to perceive in the dynamic of narration the subtle traumatic weave of the personal and the collective, the elusive nature of what wishes to name and define; in brief, the possibility and impossibility of transmission, of relating (one's own) experience.

About narration

A number of theoretical specifications are employed here. First, the conception of the subject underlying the research, in which psychoanalysis and the sciences of language come together: a fractured subject, by definition incomplete, moulded by language and whose existential dimension is *dialogic*, open to (and constructed by) an *Other*: an other that can be both the you of interlocution and the basic otherness of language, but also the idea of the Other as radical difference.

This conception owes a great deal to Bakhtin[3]; the notion of the simultaneous protagonism of the participants in a communicative act, to the extent that the essential quality of the utterance is its *addressivity*, the 'quality of being directed at someone', at an-other, the (present, absent, real or imaginary) addressee and then attending to its expectations, anticipating its objections, *responding* both in terms of *giving a response* and taking responsibility for one's own word and that of the Other, in that strong sense of 'vouching for'. So response and responsibility are intertwined in an ethical plane.

But those protagonisms do not imply being at the origin of meaning. On the contrary, the Bakhtinian conception shows more than one point of coincidence with psychoanalysis, particularly that of Lacan: the idea of a decentring of the subject with respect to language, which she enters rather than creates, occupies a place of enunciation inhabited by others' words – although she can take possession of those

words through a chosen discursive genre and the expression
of their emotion; a subject who is also decentred with respect
to the unconscious, which appears as pure antagonism, as a
self-imposed obstacle, an internal limit that impedes the reali-
zation of full identity, and where the process of the formation
of the subject – in which narratives are an essential part – can
never be more than a constantly renewed and failed attempt
to 'forget' that trauma, that constitutive lack.

Here it is possible to find one of the reasons for the constant
unfolding of biographical space, the innumerable narratives
in which the I is enunciated *for* and *through* the other – in a
variety of ways, also elliptical and masked – and in doing so
gives form – and therefore meaning – to the uncertain lives
we all lead, whose unity, as such, does not exist outside the
story. To put it another way, there is no 'subject' or 'life' that
the story represents – with the evanescence and caprice of
memory – rather, both of them (the subject and the life) are,
as an intelligible unit, the *result* of the narrative. Before that
narrative act – without it – there is only that muted murmur
of existence, disjunctive temporalities in the simultaneity
of memory, sensation, impulse and lived experience – with
its immediacy and permanency, its dazzling quality and
expressive capacity, as the monad of the universe.

From this viewpoint, the story of a life becomes a multiplicity of divergent, superimposed *histories*, none of which
can claim greater representativeness. And this is not only
valid for autobiography (capable of remaking itself several
times during the course of a life) as a genre reserved for the
celebrities of this world but also for the everyday experience
of conversation, that place in which we are all autobiographers. Because we do not always tell the same story, even
when recounting the same events: on each occasion, the
enunciative situation, the chosen discursive genre and the
other, the interlocutor, impose a form on the story and so
conform its meaning.

In the same vein, Hayden White,[4] one of the exponents
of the 'linguistic turn', would claim a role for History, with
a capital H, that is not the mere representation of events of
the past – as originals in some neutral environment – as but
a narrative and, hence, configurative: history (which history?)
is also the result of narration.

That configurative role of language is of paramount importance in the narratives discussed here: the *I* as a grammatical marker that operates in the illusory unity of the subject, the form of the story, which traces the contour of what can be spoken, leaving a trace of the inexpressible. At this limit, narrative allows for the unfolding of temporality, that *human* quality of time that cannot be perceived in the singular and which the story inscribes as the experience of the subjects. A narrative time that Paul Ricoeur[5] imagines to be consistent with *narrative identity*, as a figure of the interval, the oscillation between poles, the self (*idem*) and the other (*ipse*), between the necessary mooring of (self-)recognition and permanence, and what is changeful, open to temporality: a non-essential, relational identity whose limits are marked out in the otherness of the self.

The concept of narrative identity, applicable to both individuals and the community – family, group, nation – allows a closer analysis of *narratives* (literary, historical, memorial, biographical), considering them not only in terms of their semiotic potential (linguistic or visual) but also, particularly, in their ethical dimension, in what speaks of the vicissitudes of life, the roughness of the world and experience and, fundamentally, *of the relationship with others.*

Biography, memory

If in some way narratives of the I (self-narratives) configure us as the ephemeral subjects we are, this becomes much more perceptible in relation to memory and its aim of elaborating past traumatic experiences. There, in the difficulty of any linguistic expression of painful lived experiences, possibly partially obscured in daily life, the challenge involved in *saying again*, which the performative capacity of language makes *living again*, involves not just giving form and meaning to personal history but also a therapeutic (the need to speak, narration as working on pain) and fundamentally ethical dimension, inasmuch as it reconnects the circuit of communication – in person or in the 'absence' involved in the writing – and allows an almost corporeal *listening*, with all its signifying weight in terms of responsibility for the Other.[6] But it also allows for a setting out on the path from the individual to the collective: memory as an obligatory step towards History.

In recent decades, that long road has been characteristic of Argentina, where testimonial and autobiographical narratives have been essential to the elaboration of the experience of the last military dictatorship.[7] In the first stage, after the return to democracy in 1983, the narratives were purely testimonial: the emergence of the horror in the voices of the victims, survivors, family members, witnesses and even the repressors, brought together by a commission of notable figures from various walks of life (the National Commission on the Disappearance of Persons [CONADEP])[8] and later transformed into evidence for the juridical process. In a second stage, the memory of the militancy of the 1970s was added, recovering the political dimension, its desire for radical change, whether in terms of the activities of grassroots militant movements or in the case of the clandestine guerrilla groups.[9] In this way, other memories began to emerge, in which the figures of both the militant and the victim, often without clear distinction – or taken in their progress between rise and 'fall' – appeared, mixed with 'real' or barely fictionalized events of people in different genres and modalities: interviews, biographies, autofiction, novels with autobiographical pretensions, confessions, fictional stories unequivocally based on experience.

In this diversity of genres, even fiction with no autobiographical pretensions often took on a testimonial slant; as if to talk about that still-present past was only possible if the voice were – albeit ideally – restored to its protagonists in its immediacy, in that ground zero in which, as Derrida states, 'there is no witness for the witness'.[10] Voices that perhaps narrow the distance of experience and resist its loss, putting at centre stage the elusive figure of the narrator/storyteller whose decline, perhaps along with that of oral narrative, had so concerned Benjamin decades previously.[11]

Later, a form of cinema with a strong autobiographical influence emerged. These films often involved the children of the disappeared and ranged from classic stories that attempt to recover – or question – their parents' vanished lives and find some meaning in them to other self-referential examples elaborated with Brechtian distancing.[12]

In a third stage, more than thirty years on, these diverse memories coexist with self-criticism, with fierce debates on the political violence of the seventies – one of which will be explored in the following chapter – with a profusion of academic research that has produced an important corpus, with the creation in various cities of memory archives holding a great variety of material, including the biographical archives created by the Abuelas de Plaza de Mayo (Grandmothers of Plaza de Mayo), including a wide range of data and artefacts, to be passed on to the 'recovered' grandchildren as a first attempt at the story of their forebears' lives.[13]

The moment has also arrived to discuss public politics of memory, to create memorable sites and monuments, to open up the squalid spaces of horror, the clandestine detention centres, which were both concentration and extermination camps, many of them in the very hearts of cities – with sometimes only a thin wall separating those places of torture, humiliation and suffering from the bustle of the street, people's everyday lives, the normal coming and going between work and leisure – in order to offer an exemplary vision for those who lived through the era and for posterity. Politics of memory that are strangely consistent with the (re)opening of trials after the repeal of the laws of impunity, oral public hearings that mobilize great numbers of people, and give rise to street demonstrations, media coverage, diverging views and debates; in short, a present continuous reality that questions the denomination of 'recent history'.

So to speak of narratives of memory or places of memory is a long way from any sense of univocality, of simply referring to a conglomeration of voices or certain materialities that are there, passively accepting perception or emotion, marked by the ethical obligation of memory, which is, at this stage of civilization, almost a universal even if unequally respected duty. On the contrary, the struggle for the meaning of the events – for the meaning of history – occurs almost daily and there are different views even among those who are wholeheartedly on the side of the victims and the human rights that were so gravely violated, not to mention the 'countermemories' that, as in the famous dispute between historians in Germany, attempt to deny the existence and seriousness of the facts or justify them by drawing equivalences between the violence of armed struggle and state terrorism[14] or plead for a 'reconciled' past.

If conflict is inherent in any affirmation of collective memory, the Argentinian experience also displays the dilemmas of memory, or rather *memory as dilemma*, not only in terms of content – what it carries to the present of the utterance, the scarred bodies and souls of those who remember – but also of the forms that this evocation adopts and the insurmountable differences of viewpoint. Because it is not simply a matter of banishing remnants to oblivion, but of laboriously articulating emotion, imagination and reflection. Here the modalities of speech strongly mark the ethical dimension of what has been mentioned above: the position of the speaker, her/his role in the weave, her/his (self-)valuation, the possibility of elaboration and critical distance.

To the extent that these memories are, by definition, inexhaustible, their proliferation can also produce an opposite effect, a saturation that approaches the limit of what can be assimilated. Something of this sort has happened – or is in the process of happening – in this story that is not yet history: testimony and autobiography, whose limits expand to include every type of personal memory; the grounding in the first person that, beyond self-reference, appears as the authorized word, sufficient for historical justification. While this exacerbation does indeed merit critical analysis,[15] it can be thought that the possibly excessive emergence of those 'I's puts at stake the very figure of disappearance: the silence of destinies, the emptiness of bodies, the poverty of documents (vanished, hidden, destroyed), the stolen identities, that irreparable fracture in the very concept of community. Voices that tell of other, silenced voices whose faces follow us, addressing us from thousands of photographs, asking something of the gaze beyond remembrance: an attempt to respond in some way to that perturbing question: *How was it possible?*

But in the figure of disappearance, in that implacable logic of annihilation, there is also another singularity: the outrage at the heart of the home, violent irruption, the kidnapping or murder of parents in front of their children, and on occasions the abduction of the children, the undisguised involvement or the perpetual menace looming over families. So, on an uncertain path that began with an impossible utterance,

'Return the disappeared alive', was unfolding what could be called a *genealogical configuration of memory*: Mothers, Grandmothers, Relatives, Sons, Daughters, Brothers, Sisters, the names of the different groupings with similar concerns, in which the return of illegally taken Grandchildren was also an objective. A memory marked by family ties but with institutional backing, which is possibly a unique situation in the Latin American countries also affected by experience of dictatorship in the past or military violence in the present. In that mesh, it is not difficult to comprehend the strong identification of young people who, over and above their eventual commitment to human rights, irrupt into literature, cinema, theatre and the visual arts as the children of the disappeared, or recovered grandchildren, a denomination that in some way marks their work with inheritance and, in general, pride in that inheritance, at times tempered by the pain of absence or resentment of the fact that those parents had put their militancy before their children. In this way, artistic creation has become one of the modes of working on grief.

The biographical and testimonial imprints of these narratives, speaking of lived experience and referring to real events and people, should not allow us to forget the classic distinction between author and narrator present in the literary theory of past decades, which even includes autobiography, despite the fact that both figures can be identified in the genre. So, beyond the truth of what is narrated, the intention of authenticity or fidelity to memory – essential on the ethical plane – it is always a construction in which language or the image – or both – impose their own coordinates according to the conventions of the chosen discursive genre, and their possible infringements; this is a process of development in which other voices speak – unattended – in their own voices, subject to the insistent demands of the unconscious and the whims of memories. The narrative *I* is not necessarily autobiographical – even when it posits itself as such – and the autobiographical *I* has no legal claim to singularity however much it attempts to – and believes it does – always tell the same story: Derridian *iterability* makes that paradox of being self and other clear on every occasion, in the drift of language and temporality, in the slippage of discourse and its ungovernable appropriation in reading and listening, precisely where what is not marked, the unexpected, the relegated, silence, possibly has meaning.

Maybe what is important is to find an *I* (that narrates) rather than the *I* that flourishes on the threshold of the utterance. An *I* that lends a face to what does not have one of its own, like the rhetorical notion of *prosopopoeia* that Paul de Man[16] associates with autobiography: a mask that occupies the place of an absence, that endows what was not previously an *I* with a face and voice. In other words, *an* I *that is nothing more than its own representation.*

Those theoretical defences that do not question the validity of testimony as subjective truth, evidence for an accusation or documentation, allow a vision, in that multiplication of narratives, of lack – those who are not there – as a symptom and the repeated digressions through which trauma, traumatic experience, attempts to speak the unspeakable, what evades symbolization, the remnant, *the Real*, in Lacanian terms. An exacerbated 'telling everything' because 'everything' cannot be told.

There is in that 'telling everything' the terrifying detail of torture, rape, suffering. A detail that, far from being morbid, is established in the need for proof in a trial, attestation of the crime for the intervention of the justice system, and also a historical document. At this point, the testimonies of the survivors of the Argentinian camps are close to those of Nazi Germany. Brought to speak, beyond the imperious need to reconfigure a devastated subjectivity, in order to testify to things they are the only witnesses to – the body as evidence – to what exceeds the possibilities of the imagination and leaves questions unanswered: that human aptitude for cruelty, ridicule, humiliation, the violation of all boundaries. In the testimonies, there is a notable presence of that wealth of detail, which even crosses thresholds of modesty or prudery and responds to both the veridiction contract of the testimony – proof of a truth that can be *incredible* – and self-restoration in the face of the guilt of having survived.

That final aspect, linked to a form of social suspicion of survival (particularly among militants), is a recurrent theme in the stories. The figure of the traitor – the person who agreed to 'collaborate' with the repressor and so saved her/his life – is as present in testimony as in fiction,[17] although with gradations: the people who were forced to undertake certain tasks in the concentration camps, those who formed sexual or amorous relationships with the repressor, those who openly switched sides.[18] In many cases, unmitigated moral censure wins out over a more objective evaluation, particularly in relation to experiences at the limits: the degree to which free will and resolution can be exercised in captivity, under constant threat of death, in conditions of extreme uncertainty. Experiences which formed part of that 'precarious life', to use Judith Butler's[19] expression, in which not only was torture repeated innumerable times and the conditions were inhumane, but where there was also no possibility of foreseeing the future, of knowing on any particular day the who or why of being 'transferred' (a euphemism for death).

The extreme experience of the camps could then be narrated by the survivors. Some had had the option of leaving the country; others had been offered stepped liberation under vigilance. Beyond the testimonies (which on the return to democracy produced the *Never Again* report), many of which were repeated during the long sessions of the Juicio a las ex Juntas Militares (Trial of the Juntas) in 1985, that memory has its posterity, which has continued to flourish over the years and has been translated into a variety of narratives. Perhaps due to gender solidarity or because they ask the most pressing questions, I am particularly interested here in the writings of certain women.

Being at the limit

To be received, a testimony must be appropriated, that is, divested as much as possible of the absolute foreignness that horror engenders.

Paul Ricoeur (2004)[20]

There are various moments in the process of the unfolding of testimony in which the word becomes audible, can be spoken and heard. Moments that are close to the lived events, which show themselves as urgencies of the voice; and others that, whether from fear, anguish, shame or desperation, are more distanced. Temporalities of memory that resist the subjection of chronological ordering, what a certain political logic considers the time needed to remember.

The testimonies of women subjected to torture, conflict-related violence or repression often require a greater degree of this distancing, insofar as that violence inevitably involves humiliation of the body, sexual abuse and rape, topics not easily addressed in public. However, many women testified to those atrocious experiences at an early stage, both from exile, in the *Nunca Más* report, or during the trials of the former Juntas Militares.[21]

In a number of cases, these stories were later set down in individual or collective works that, without losing their testimonial character, crossed over into other discursive genres: essays, life stories, conversations, letters, poetic texts, autofiction. From a large corpus that offers certain similarities,[22] I am particularly interested in two works that show differences in terms of their discursive genres and modes of enunciation, each of which is unique in its own way: Pilar Calveiro's *Poder y desaparición. Los campos de concentración en Argentina* [*Power and Disappearance. Concentration Camps in Argentina*],[23] where the story of the experience takes the form of a PhD thesis, with all that such a work demands, and *That Inferno: Conversations of Five Women Survivors of an Argentine Torture Camp*,[24] a book co-authored by Munú Actis, Cristina Aldini, Liliana Gardella, Miriam Lewis and Elisa Tokar, in which conversations held during a number of encounters not associated with declarations attempt to (re)construct a shared memory.[25]

Testimony can be considered as a type of autobiography in which two imaginaries of truth and reality are united (and reinforce each other): the events that took place and the experience they provoke. Once again, however, it is not a matter of the pure expression of the lived experience but of the unfolding of language in a narrative configuration involving certain strategies of self-representation: how to construe to narrative *I*, its qualities, attributes, circumstances, values, the perception of time, its chronology – the order of events that are often freed from the organization of the story; the words and events that are remembered and, of course, the gender markers.

In the first of these works, Pilar Calveiro, living in exile in Mexico, chooses to address the experience of the concentration camp in a political sciences PhD thesis. She undertakes an analysis of causes, consequences, modalities, routines, institutional logistics, historicity, behaviours and actions, and from this she constructs a political critique in which the strong hypothesis is that concentration camps do not come into existence in just any society, that they are not simply the (extreme) product of a repressive apparatus, but they arise from a *concentrationary power* whose potential conditions are present within the society itself and its indissoluble other. Following the conventions of academic writing, which give preference to a distancing from subjectivity, Calveiro avoids the enunciative *I* (the only reference to her personal experience in the camp is a mention, of her ESMA[26] identification number, given among others at the beginning of the text: '... Pilar Calveiro: 362')[27] – digressing in *débrayage*, in the third person – or 'non-person', as Benveniste[28] terms it – and at no time involves herself as one of the characters in the story. She replaces herself with the testimonies of other people – detained-disappeareds, survivors – who bear witness in full detail to the terrifying development of that 'periodic table', in Primo Levi's words, and in this way includes the voices of those suffered under it.

> These are stories of what was known in the Escuela de Mecánica de la Armada, 'on the transfer days, strict security measures were put in place and the basement was isolated. The prisoners had to stay in their cells in silence. At about 17:00 hours every Wednesday, the people to be transferred were designated, and they were taken one by one to the infirmary, just as they were, dressed or half-undressed, in the heat or cold.'[29]

> The atmosphere was very tense on the transfer days. We didn't know if it was going to be our turn ... the detainees were called by number ... They were escorted to the infirmary in the basement, where the nurse was waiting to give the injections to make them sleep, but not kill them. So, still alive, they were taken out a side door of the basement and put in a truck. In a fairly deep sleep they were driven to the Aeroparque, loaded into a plane that flew south into the sea, where they were thrown out alive ... Captain Acosta at first banned any reference to the topic of 'transfers'.[30]

Calveiro's stance could be interpreted as a form of Bakhtinian *extra-position*,[31] in which the author distances herself from the character, situates herself outside looking in – as was in fact geographically and existentially the case – so as to then compose the warp and weft of the story without autobiography's ever-latent risk of self-satisfaction or self-commiseration, although not of course without the effects of that painful task on personal subjectivity.

> The nudity, the hood hiding the face, the bonds and gags, the pain and the loss of all personal possessions, were signs of initiation into this world where all the proprieties, norms, values, logics of the outside seemed to be annulled, and where human feeling itself seemed to have been suspended. The prisoner's nudity and the hood increase vulnerability but also express a desire to make his intimacy clear to the violated man, to take possession of his secret, to watch him without being seen, a desire that lies beneath the torture and constitutes one of the 'house rules'.[32]

This would also appear to demonstrate Maurice Blanchot's affirmation that 'there is more intensity' and possibly greater ethical acceptability 'in the sentence "he[she] suffers" than "I suffer"'.[33] The digression from the *I* to the third person – which is emblematically marked in Barthes' autobiography *Roland Barthes by Roland Barthes*[34] – locates intimate experience in another dimension, lowering the emotional tone to leave space for theoretical and political reflection, a gesture that to some extent also supposes a critical attitude to self-reference. The ethical act implied by all testimony has here to do with distancing and retention, with the anti-heroic gesture of privileging experience as a means of elucidation and understanding of the events rather than an end in itself or a justification of the account. Thus, with the addition of the scientific rigour of the third-person voice, it has been transformed into an obligatory reference for any analytical approach to the events of that ill-fated decade.

From a different perspective, the book by the five women, also survivors of the ESMA, assumes the most classically autobiographical *I*, where the subjective emphasis features prominently, although woven into a group account. In this sense, it also posits a singularity: that of the testimony of several voices, woven into the logic of everyday conversation in periodic meetings, very different from a statement given in court and so as evidence (each of the authors had given legal testimony at the appropriate time, some while living abroad, soon after being released, others during the trials of the ex-juntas or shortly afterwards), very different from any petition, except the restless urge – need? – to return more than twenty years later to that traumatic experience, from an *I* that remembers step by step and pares down its personal pain in dialogue with others, a *we*, even when the vocative is not strongly marked in the interventions; that is to say, from a collective genre that marks the text and its reading from the very first pages. In this sense, it is perhaps a more complete attempt to narrate a shared history literally 'from the inside', to attest to the routine character of the camp, with its chiaro-scuro, in an existential narrative that exceeds the limits of testimony as juridical evidence.

What is it that leads one, after so much time, to return to the past? Why make the most intimate experience of fear, humiliation, torture and pain public? Why relive each instance of suffering: abduction, confinement, torture, denun-ciation, sexual abuse, perversion, the loss of companions, the fear of death, exile? Because language inexorably carries with it the full weight of emotion.

Calveiro's book, also published twenty years after the events, seemed to respond in advance to those questions: the return to the past as a contribution to theory and criticism, from a perspective that is both distanced and restorative: the renunciation of the *I*, that frees protagonism and traumatic revelation from intimacy; the lived events, but as lived by many, so that they transcend the singularity of biography to become, beyond the 'memory', a historical wound, an ineradicable mark in the ethical space of the collective.

The five female narrators considered here also in some way anticipate their responses in the rationales that form a prelude to the book: they refer to the temporality of memory that has only recently allowed them, so many years later, to return to reflect on the recollections and lived experiences lying dormant in a recovered normality but which resurface at certain moments with squalid, menacing overtones. They take the decision to 'limit [their] group to women', recognizing the difficulty of speaking of the devastated intimacy that had specific gender-related characteristics: 'nudity and humiliation, sexual harassment by our repressors, relationships with our pregnant *compañeras* and their children. For our male *compañeros*, the time spent in the ESMA undoubtedly evoked different types of feelings.'[35] They respect the friendship that grew between them in such horrendous conditions and the shared desire to leave a record of their experiences that goes beyond what has been said on other occasions, the desire to fill the gaps of the parts of the story they were not fully aware of. They value the support involved in talking as a group and in laughter and teasing as antidotes to fright. They accept that during the three years of their meetings there were painful moments, reopened wounds, tears, doubts, uncertainties and desolation, and that the achievement of the final product, the book, could never have been foreseen at the outset. In short, the initiative is at once a form of group catharsis and a direct, testimonial contribution to knowledge of the lived experience of that state of exception.

In addition to the topics addressed in that long conversation, to the events and people it introduces (some of them well known, coinciding with other testimonies, biographical or fictional stories), and given that it is in fact a *text*, a worked piece of writing, what interests me here, as might be expected, is the issue of language, discourse and narration. What did the speakers do to language and, perhaps more disturbingly, what did language do to them? What were their strategies of self-representation? What gender markers – if any – appear in the story of the traumatic experience? What silences appear in the discourse, its blind spots, its vacillations?

This analysis, then, attempts to add, however modestly, to the discussion on the uses of testimony (the 'to speak or not to speak'), the appropriateness of 'returning to the past' and, possibly, the limits of what can be said when one has undergone an experience at the limit.

Testimony as conversation: it could be a hypothetical title for this book. On the one hand, it once again affirms the therapeutic, socializing and revelatory aspects of our pre-eminent communicative practice; on the other, it introduces the lightness of colloquial speech, its familiar turns and everyday expressions in another mode of speech that is located far from that everyday life. Two almost opposing genres whose confluence results in an other-form, a problematic alloy. Not because the flow of voices carries humour, or encourages optimism in the darkest moments (its therapeutic function) but due to the divergence of tones and styles, the distance between the thing said and the act of saying, between the minutiae of everyday life in the camp with its anecdotes and the awful environment in which they occur, between the horror of *That Inferno* in all its detail, the tortured bodies and souls and the smooth progression of the – appropriately edited – conversation, with no trace of silences, hesitations, wearied voices ...[36] A forced remembering, a 'saying it all' in a continuous flow of words which seems to wish to leave nothing out, and which for that reason can be read as a symptom.

Because if it is true that, as theory has it, trauma is located beyond language but at the same time needs it, language itself – what language? – may be the intrinsic dilemma of testimony. As Leigh Gilmore points out: 'Survivors of trauma are urged to testify repeatedly to their trauma in an effort to create the language that will manifest and contain trauma as well as the witnesses who will recognize it.'[37] It is, then, a matter of replacing the manifestations through which the unconscious initially 'speaks' (flashbacks, night-mares, emotional outbursts) with a conscious language that repeatedly attempts to speak of what cannot be spoken. An apparent contradiction in terms that involves a fundamental ambivalence: the possibility and impossibility of language for giving expression to trauma.

But, in addition to a language, testimony requires an appropriate (juridical, institutional) framing to carry out its task; an *other*, prepared to listen and retain and to do this while subjected to a strong demand for veracity and trust-worthiness, but also legality, in the case of accusations of false testimony.

In the environment of the conversation, as it is constructed in the text, in which the authors' responses alternate fluidly, flow – and contradict one another – traces of several discursive genres coexist: testimony, autobiography and confession in a narrative articulation replete with stylistic devices (description, temporality, evoked scenes and characters, reproduction of dialogue in direct speech, the imagining of situations or the supposed endings of stories, etc.) that could be defined as forms of collective autofiction.

In terms of testimony, the statements, while outside the canonical frame of declarations to a court, do however attempt to give an account of the events and characters, keeping strictly to the principle of truth, and can be immediately corroborated to the extent that they refer to situations experienced by all the women. The interlocutors then interrupt the (testimonial) *hearing* to again become witnesses – in the double sense of giving testimony of what has been *lived* and what has been *seen*, a distinction which is clear in the narrative.[38] In terms of autobiography, while the text does not achieve an articulated outline of the lives of each of the participants, there are fragments of those lives, anecdotes, feelings, character traces and, consequently, empathy between the participants in the conversation; 'autobiographical moments', as Paul de Man would call them, that figure which 'happens as an alignment between the two subjects involved in the process of reading [the narrator, the reader] in which they determine each other by mutual reflexive substitution'.[39] A figure which, according to de Man, is not exclusive to autobiography but can appear in any text, and which, in *this* text, operates in spectacular triangulation: we are, as readers, third parties included in a conversation, which, moreover, shows certain shared genre-related features.[40] But, in the back-and-forth of conversation, there are also moments that could be called 'confessional' in which something of what has not been (perhaps has never been) said suddenly surfaces and then sinks back. This is also a common occurrence in everyday conversation: something that arises unbidden in the logic of language, as if emerging from the unconscious or because it has yet to be precisely formulated. Listening once again reveals itself – in the scene of writing – as essential to the construction of the subject and, thus, to life.

Liliana: Now I realize that when I was inside I felt as if they
             had installed a glass window that separated me

from the world. I knew that my name wasn't worth as much as before; it was a disappeared name.

Elisa: I'd never be able to find a term that could explain what happened to me or to describe it in any way. My name in the militant organization was Monica. When they took me to work at the Foreign Ministry,[41] there was another woman there with the same name, and when somebody said Monica, we'd both answer. I was Elisa Tokar, but I was still Monica.

Liliana: They must have thought you were crazy.

Munú: And you would explain that they called you Moni ...

Elisa: I told them that they called me Moni, short for *monigote* [ragdoll] [laughter] ...

Miriam: You identified the name Moni with the militant organization and with being inside.

Elisa: Sure, in the Foreign Ministry I was still kidnapped, and so I was still Moni; I answered to that name.[42]
             [...]

Munú: For me, those years seem so long. You talk about one thing or another, and in the interim it seems as if years had gone by. Speaking of identity, I don't know what your experience was, what it meant to you – the fact that they gave us each a number and used it to identify us.

Miriam: The number thing didn't really bother me that much.

Elisa: Me neither.

Miriam: I was 090.

Elisa: It made me feel more comfortable. I was 481. When I went in or out of Capucha[43] or they took me on an *expedition*,[44] they said '481!' It was good for me because I needed to feel that I was a prisoner. It was a way of distancing myself from the naval officers.

Munú: The need for bars!

Elisa: The famous bars we didn't have![45]

The bars (which did exist in other camps) are mentioned again later:

Elisa: She said [referring to a *compañera* in another camp]
             the bars helped her to keep her sanity. She talked
             about the symbolic bars that defined who was who.
             The jailer was the jailer.

Munú: They were always trying to distort the situation.
             They'd come, they'd beat you to a pulp with a stick,
             and then at two in the morning they'd get you, put
             you in a car, and take you out to dinner. They'd sit
             you down at the same table, turn you into an equal:
             you ate the same food, they wanted to hear your
             opinions, and then back to the Capucha you went.
             That would drive anybody crazy. Except for us!
             [Laughter][46]

In what relates specifically to the dynamic of the conversation, which is, in the end, the discursive genre that
contains the others, their 'adoptive country', although the
book is organized in chapters that attempt to sift through
a problematic issue, and the participants' responses seem to
respect a polite, turn-taking order (a topic beloved of United
States conversationalists[47]), the story constantly transgresses
these limitations; the interruptions and disruptions leave the
course of the conversation open, an openness that is the very
essence of conversation.

What strategies are brought to bear in self-representation?
How are enunciative positions constructed? If there are
indeed differences between the five female authors (emphasis,
tone and style) a common line can be seen, possibly the result
of the editing process but which entails a shared position.
Beyond the assumption of an unconditional *I*, beyond the
broad unfolding of subjectivity, the common obsession with
the details of the story of their sufferings is perfectly clear,
appearing as an insistence on information and evidence
(witnessed, testimonial and juridical) but also, it might be
thought, on *proof as tests* that, as with characters in an epic,
have been met and overcome. It is perhaps interesting to
remember here the concept of 'qualifying test' that Greimas[48]
posited, based on the classic functions of the folktale in
Propp's[49] typology: the test (facing the innumerable aspects
of adversity with the courage, mettle and virtue needed
to pass) as an obligatory step in the movement of the

hero/heroine, with his/her aides and opponents, towards maturity, wisdom, power or justice, an obligatory corollary to the eternal struggle between Good and Evil. Something of that ancient heritage persists in the five women's story, investing it, perhaps inadvertently, with a heroic nature, but leads to consideration of the multiple forms assumed by heroism, beyond typical, often tragic figures. The women have succeeded in surviving, in being undeterred by torture, by physical, psychological and moral suffering, the perversion of their repressors,[50] fear and despair. They have, however painfully, remade their lives (to use a popular expression) by frustrating the ultimate aim of concentration camp power: the destruction of subjectivity and any form of dignity. But perhaps in that dazzling accumulation of evidence verging on the excessive, one can again read the symptomatic, the persistence of a traumatic trace.

There is, of course, the guilt of survival, as was mentioned above and expressed throughout this book, a sense of guilt which perhaps unconsciously seeks to find some form of equivalence with the memory of what has been suffered. There is also the ethical commitment to *making known* that all those who have gone through the concentration camp experience share. But in terms of the story of the experience(s) of women, there are certain additional aspects worthy of consideration from the viewpoint of gender.

There is little doubt of the importance of women's autobiography (and, in general, the assumption of the first person in stories of a confessional and testimonial nature) in the construction of the epistemological fields of the various forms of feminism, gender and sexual difference studies and, from these perspectives, in the necessary redefinition of the concepts of gender, identity, agency and experience. Traumatic experience quite rightly finds a privileged mode of expression in these areas at a time when, as Leigh Gilmore[51] asserts, the eras of memories (memoirs) and trauma appear to have coincided over a period of thirty years, encouraging a multiplicity of stories in the widest range of language and formats (media, anthropological, cinema, artistic) and simultaneously giving rise to renewed critical debate about the subject, language, narration and the very notion of experience.[52] Rather than some notion of 'female experience',

which would return us to essentialism, it is a matter of
thinking of the experiences of women, with their similarities
and differences, as the product of what, in the words of
Teresa de Lauretis, can be called the 'technologies of gender';
that is to say, the social, semiotic, epistemological and critical
weave in which gendered subjects are constructed.[53]

Eschewing generalizations, then, it would seem that the
detailing of the personal misfortunes underlying the five
women's strategies of self-representation may repeat a formula
that consistently appears in other environments and writings,
although not necessarily in relation to traumatic experience.
The literary critic Rita Felski,[54] for example, points out that
many female feminist writers adopt a confessional style to
produce an authentic *self*, circumventing theory and basing
subjectivity on the personal details of lived experience. In her
opinion, this results in a 'naive' enunciative position. Leigh
Gilmore,[55] in contrast, believes that in the employment of
confessional discourse, women affirm a subjective positioning
that gives them the authority to vindicate their truth.[56]

However, in the case of the five authors discussed here,
the detailed testimony of traumatic experience that seems to
be the motive for and objective of the book plays a different
role to testimony before a court. There, the aim would be to
bear witness in the trial and conviction of victimizers from
the viewpoint of the *victims*. Here, the women give evidence
from another place, whose authority is constructed on the
story itself: the story of *survivors*. But that signifier, which
is highlighted in the subtitle of the book, is not a passive
reference to the indelible mark of the past – the fact of having
resisted, having escaped the concentration camp power with
its arbitrary handing out of death. Rather, as has been seen,
it acquires an active sense in the present: that of having
superimposed on its devastating effects the will to remember,
the authority to speaking; in brief, the assumption of a space
of agency[57] into which identity, truth and power are woven.
This is a place sustained by the *name*, resting on the return of
the *nom de guerre* of militancy and the number that attempts
to erase it, a name marked by a genealogy that was also
endangered.[58] A place, moreover, that is shared, where the
voices mutually reinforce each other in the reaffirmation of
what is said and operate as guarantors of truth.

This relational character assumed and explicitly foregrounded by the enunciation seems to support the views of certain feminist critics who believe that metonymy, the trope of contiguity and relationship, is preferred in the figurative self-representation of women in autobiography (always in relation with others) in contrast to the men, who prefer metaphor, the trope of substitution, which operates on the associative/paradigmatic axis and connotes hierarchy and identity.[59] If this does indeed translate into two opposed modes of self-representation, Gilmore reflects,[60] that difference would extend beyond rhetoric to acquire a political dimension, although, as we know, rhetoric is political. Politics, in the account discussed here, necessarily becomes a politics of memory.

If the body is traditionally excluded from autobiography (which tends towards states of the soul, the intellect, spirit and memory), in these types of accounts it appears to be intrinsically involved, not only as the object of torture but also as a mode of self-affirmation. Nevertheless, it is no easy task to carry into the narrative present scenes that one shudders just to think of, that involve the iconic power of the word that *shows itself* according to the dictates of each perception: scenes that leave the most traumatic marks. But if their enunciation is difficult – the difficulty of inserting the voice and the word into a place where language is lacking – the place in which it positions the addressee of that enunci-ation is also problematic, an addressee who is in some way positioned as a voyeur on crossing the threshold of what she/ he does not even want to imagine. This is the classic 'to see or not to see' dilemma that repeatedly appears in relation to the traumatic image and, in particular, the terrifying images of Nazi extermination camps. If – as Didi-Huberman[61] asserts in a classic polemic related to the 'four pieces of film snatched from hell' to which he ventured to add a fictional story – 'to know, we must imagine for ourselves', then testimony requires the almost obligatory exercise of the imagination. Yet that knowing supposes not just knowledge but also reflection, a response, an ethical positioning that exceeds the compassionate, salutary or even admiring impact that can be produced by the account of suffering: any form of suffering.

It is perhaps here, in the assembly of the most crudely 'feminine' – the sexual, carnal, imaginary that corporeality covers – that the five authors' narrative comes up against the greatest enunciative difficulty: the desire to bear witness with the realistic detail of juridical evidence but beyond the margins of the appropriate environment for that task and beyond the margins of the discursive genre that would support it.

And at this point we return to the issue of language: language does not merely express the experience but *takes possession* of it, configures it in the *here and now* of the enunciation, that event which, according to Benveniste,[62] makes the emergence of an *I* possible, an *I* that in turn installs – addresses – a *you*, so opening the intersubjective circuit of communication. But no *I* speaks outside a discursive genre or, it could be added, says the same thing in every genre.

The point is that every discursive genre carries, together with the thematic, compositional and stylistic norms of its utterances, a system for giving value to the world, linked to history and tradition. In this way, recognition of genres, their different forms (drama, comedy, testimony, autobiography and the novel) is not only related to their formal structure but also – and principally – to the impact that the value system has on the plane of reception and comprehension and, consequently, on the way in which it *responds* to the expectations of the addressee, in the twofold sense of response and responsibility, what Bakhtin calls the 'ethical act'.[63] Autobiography and testimony, for example, ideally comply with a principle of truth telling that does not apply to the novel or other genres that have licence to invent. Everyday conversation can be distinguished from the journalistic interview by the institutional nature of the latter, its participants and – sometimes – its themes but especially by the 'reading contract' of truth and objectivity that underpins – also ideally – the information genre. The concept of biographical value mentioned earlier lies within this ethical register.

However, and beyond the value imprint traditionally linked with them, genres are spaces of heterogeneity and hybridization and even accept borrowings, migrations and contaminations: everyday dialogue in the novel, for example, an anecdote in a scientific paper, a parody of a political speech. They also mingle by infringing their ill-defined limits and so construct spaces for new genres (or 'outside genres': the reality show, autofiction, the subjective documentary, the blog ...), each of which will, in turn, generate its own value system and communication circuit. Those borrowings, migrations or contaminations take on the form, and hence meaning, imposed on them by their adoptive territory: everyday dialogue in the novel is *novel*, yet in a news bulletin it is information. A more complex situation is found in the confluence of neighbouring genres that share certain characteristics but are radically different in others.

Such is the case of *Conversations*, where testimony, autobiography and confession necessarily form a single flow in the genre chosen by the five authors to put traumatic experience into words. But that interchange of speech, with its attempts to retain the cadence and fluidity of a clear conviviality, and which even has moments of 'women's chatter', with its humour and triviality, its evident reparative power, cannot evade that fundamental tension already noted here: the distance between the thing said and the act of saying, between the terrifying detail of this type of testimony and the form adopted by the utterance.

Given this asymmetry, the conversation can be considered as a mode of appropriation – returning to Bloch's epigraph in this section – in which, in the long term, with the restraint and companionship of equals, the collective account of horror unburdened of its 'otherness' can flourish. The question is if this outcome is finally achieved, if the chosen modality in fact makes the horror more bearable or once again highlights the limit of what can be said, its radical otherness.

Underlying this question is the fact that conversation which has been transcribed, edited and passed into writing loses its immediacy, its *primacy*, and becomes a secondary, more developed genre – following Bakhtinian theory – the product of an elaboration of language that operates at a distance from the voice (stress, intonation and emotion) in a process of loss, of entropy. This genre has a long journalistic and literary tradition: books of 'conversations' with celebrities, writers, poets, philosophers and scientists. But in those cases the dialogue is closer to the model of the interview than everyday conversation, and a speculative relationship often exists between interviewer and interviewee; there is a person who attempts to construct an image of him/herself, or a portrait in which private life is woven to varying extents with the assertion or the creative act in an attempt to demonstrate the uncertain articulation between art and life that so interested Bakhtin.[64]

In these 'conversations', which could also be considered 'outside genre', the aim is quite different and perhaps their ambivalence – or otherness – finally depends on the models of reception. Once catharsis has been enacted, far from the supposed spontaneity of speech, *the book returns to speak*, takes on the challenge of visibility, of exposing the most recondite intimacy to the interrogating light of the public sphere and, as an utterance, is directed at someone and responds – in advance – to its interrogators and their expectations. The questions that arise in relation to any writing are again pertinent here. For whom is one writing? Who is the addressee the text hopes to *respond* to, the addressee for whom discourse takes ethical responsibility?

(In)Conclusions

If the biographical, the private or intimate spheres construct hypothetical thresholds to the profundity of the *I*, a gradation in which the biographical can be public without the trace of privacy, and the private can become public without the trace of intimacy, then intimacy can, on occasions, disregard the tempered steps of that gradation and irrupt into the public sphere with a violence of the word that possibly exceeds the image (although in fact the word is image). It is the violence of testimony in the traumatic denuding of intimacy subjected to torture, in the fateful detail of the injury meted out to bodies, that 'bare life' which appears without biographical contours, without even the mantle of privacy.

Those testimonies, with their phantasmal horror, their nightmare corollary, have gradually populated the successive weaves of memory, from the *Never Again* and the later trials of the former military juntas to the present day, in the oral and public trials still taking place. But outside the witness stands, the institutional framework, those stories re-emerge with – following my hypothesis – symptomatic insistence to insert words into that place where so many voices are lacking and language fails, and the possibility of speaking the truth once again reaches its limits. However, when accommodated in other narratives (autobiographies, life stories, interviews, letters, photographs, hybrids of fiction and non-fiction[65]), they no longer say the same thing. They can speak without the dispossession of legal proof, with the perspective of distance or the refuge of interlocution, under the protection of biography, happy memories, life *before* or the strength of survival, with the support of metaphor, the imagination, humour or political thought. And it is undoubtedly literature that has had greatest success in working on modes of enunciation as a way of recovering the mantle, of clothing bareness, of once again discovering the poetic dimension of existence.[66]

The narratives I have analysed here attempt, in their different ways, to offer testimony a mantle: the mantle of theory and critical reflection in the case of Calveiro; that of conviviality and conversation in the work of the five female authors. Both these examples move away from the most common form of the testimonial voice – the singular, self-referential account of hardships – and, insofar as they extend the space of what can be said, take on new challenges in their enunciation: the demarcation of the third person in an academic discourse that excludes personal subjectivity; the assumption of a polyphonic positioning that multiplies subjectivities.

As stated above, language takes possession of experience, not the reverse. And the discursive genre chosen to give an account of that experience configures it not only in terms of its formal, compositional and stylistic elements but, above all, of the value system that underlies it, the intersubjective relationship it posits – the particular place it assigns to both the speaker and the addressee – and therefore the ways in which utterances respond to the promise each discourse entails.

The promise of truth and trustworthiness that characterizes testimony is fulfilled, in different ways, in both the thesis and the conversations. They share a narrative function; the former with greater strength of argument, the latter with a clearer subjective stress. So, the experience of the two 'events' (that will never be the same experience) can be told in modes that are opposing yet, I would venture, complementary. In the case of Calveiro, as has been pointed out, the aim of the narrative is to use a piece of research that employs theory and documentary sources to demonstrate the ways in which concentration camp power is structured and reinforced. And it does this without renouncing the expression of the lived experience of those who suffered under that system, bringing together other voices – of men and women – and their testimony. The assumption of the third person – precluding the baring of personal intimacy as it exposes the utterance to debate and discussion, both of which might be left unspoken in a self-referential voice – is accompanied by a curious demarcation: it is the male gender – 'men', 'the man' – that always seems to be alluded to in the argument as an active subject or victim of the concentration camp experience.

The five female authors, for their part, add to the account of the events a dimension committed to traumatic experience, the gaze, from the 'inside', which is also an immersion in personal subjectivity. In this sense, they bear witness through their own example to the mechanisms of cruelty analysed in the PhD thesis – which in turn adds theoretical and argumentative support to the 'conversations'. This discursive option, in proximity to the lived experience, that sheds light on moments and circumstances that would otherwise perhaps be hidden in more distanced stories, does, however, involve certain risks: the overflowing of intimate spaces – in times of the barrage of media intimacy – and the chance development of conversation, which could leave the imprint of the everyday on even the most sensitive moments of an evocation, in some way naturalizing what was a liminal experience in a state of exception.

Analysed from the perspective of gender, both interventions, in their different ways, construct a site of agency. The thesis, despite its impersonal enunciation, reaffirms the possibility of the author speaking of a traumatic experience from the basis of a rational approach, a genre that is neither autobiographical nor confessional, both of which are often considered to be characteristic of writing by women. The 'conversations', for their part, as I already mentioned, resist the temptation of 'victimization' to take on the authority

– the freedom – of a self-reflexive, at times ironic, utterance, of an affirmation of the *person* (denied, in captivity) in her multiple dimensions.

Despite their differences, in both cases language – writing – gives form to experience, proposes a non-existent coherence in life, a chronology, a *mise en intrigue* – with the addition of a level of suspense – in which the desire for the real organizes into history what was fragmentary and overlapping, a provisional organization that other voices will come to disrupt in the unceasing development of the stories that 'witness literature', according to Hayden White, and that will always leave a trace of what cannot be expressed.

5

Political Violence,
Autobiography and Testimony[1]

In recent years, possibly confirming that any collective elaboration of a traumatic past contains temporalities of memory,
a variety of narratives have appeared in Argentina, related to
the political violence of the 1970s, which bear witness to the
terrible experience of repression unleashed by the last military
dictatorship (1976–1983), adding to the debate, remembrance
or fiction of the *guerrillera* experience both in the initial
stages of the campaign in the north of the country in the early
seventies and in the period of urban radicalization, before
and after the passage into clandestinity of the armed groups
that were consolidated in the following decade: the Ejército
Revolucionario del Pueblo (People's Revolutionary Army),
the Fuerzas Armadas Revolucionarias (Revolutionary Armed
Forces) and the left-wing Peronist group, the Montoneros.

In these narratives, there is a strong presence of personal
experience, an *I* that narrates from the most canonical
autobiographical genres or the testimony of those who
have lived, seen or heard but also from different fictional or
autofictional exercises that, freed from the need to confine
themselves to events, their exact dating or the veracity of
situations and people, allow for the appearance of socially
reprehensible behaviours, 'prohibited' emotions; in short,
show perhaps more crudely the boundary line between the
public and private, between the epic and the intimate.

One of the most notable examples to be found among the non-fiction narratives in this problematic area is a unique corpus of debate around the *guerrillero* militancy generated by an interview with Héctor Jouvé, one of the leading figures and survivors of the Guevara guerrillas. When the interview was published in the Córdoba magazine *La Intemperie*, it provoked a heated letter from the philosopher Oscar del Barco under the epigraph '*No matarás*' ('Thou shalt not kill'). From there, a long and profuse correspondence was unleashed between intellectuals, writers, psychoanalysts, thinkers and former militants, which was collected in an initial 500-page tome entitled *No matar. Sobre la responsibilidad* (*No Killing: On Responsibility*),[2] whose arguments in turn inspired a variety of essays by other authors, compiled in a second volume.[3] The reflections that follow refer exclusively to the first volume.

That long debate[4] was, naturally, never settled. There were too many thorny issues involved: the relationship between politics and violence; the very conception of violence and its possible division into 'good' and 'bad' forms – or, rather, the violence of the oppressed and of the oppressors; the questioning of the actions of the guerrilla forces and also their justification of historical circumstance – the historical 'alibi', its elitist character, divorced from the masses (in the Argentinian experience) and also the recovery of its ideals; the difficult distinction between means and ends; the validity of the very idea of revolution and the ideals related to it; and, fundamentally, past and present responsibility in terms of activities in which death – on one side or the other, that is, killing and dying – was a constant possibility.

Passionate and also violent – that violence of writing that both Derrida and Barthes perceived so clearly – the debate, undoubtedly the most important that has arisen to date, opened old wounds, uncovered silences, forgetting, taboos, grievances, deceptions and, more disturbingly, the enormous difficulty (for some, the impossibility) of assuming a critical and self-critical evaluation of responsibility for one's own life and the lives of others. Rather than answers – despite the fact that an attempt was made to give them from a variety of viewpoints – the debate sowed doubts, questions and nuclei of meaning of the order of the undecidable.

My interest in addressing this debate is not to offer an exegesis of its arguments – however intricate – or weigh up the different positions in the dispute but to attempt to read it as a symptom: a symptom of the disillusion, disorientation, the 'state of the soul' – if I may be allowed the expression – of the present-day left-wing intellectual field, of what was still to be addressed in the elaboration of the past, of the inherent conflict involved in the (retrospective) definition of an ethics of responsibility. But since it is a discursive event – writing on violence – I also want to consider the genres involved, their ethics, performativity and rhetoric, the modes of installation of an *I* and the ways in which individual experience – biography – intervenes in the conceptualization of a historical moment.

The tone of the debate

What caused such a commotion? What was the motive behind del Barco's letter and the fierce reactions it awakened? In his interview, Héctor Jouvé revived the awful experiences of the guerrilla group he was a member of – the Ejército Guerrillero del Pueblo (People's Guerrilla Army) – that, filled with revolutionary zeal, had penetrated the north of Argentina in the hope of making contact with certain figures close to Che (Guevara) who were then being trained in Bolivia. It is an unembellished story of the adventures of middle-class, urban youths lost in the immensity of the wilds of Salta province, crossing unknown terrain, facing hunger, an inclement climate, the suspicion of local people, without any clear orientation, objective or meaning to their actions. The narrator retraces that journey, recovering emblematic scenes (the attempt to make contact with guerrilla groups in Bolivia, occasional meetings with local families, periods with little or no food, the discovery of the tracks of border forces, the later disbanding of the group, his capture and imprisonment) which are interspersed with a critical evaluation of the group's activities and political comment, plus leaps into the present. It is a narrative that could be compared with an adventure story – without a clear plot or ending – but which, nevertheless, includes one very serious matter: the 'execution' of two of his companions, one supposedly 'broken', the other suspected of endangering the safety of the group, deaths he had firmly opposed and still mourned. With its modesty, simplicity and lack of self-pity, Jouvé's testimony was not presented as an exercise of memory – or in memoriam; rather, possibly with the distance of the Benjaminian chronicler, it was burdened with the imperishable weight of that experience in the present (the weight of guilt or, more precisely, responsibility), with the intention of adding to reflection on the situation and generating responses, also in the present.

Of course, that was not the first time that the issue had been brought up. In the long-term memory, during the forty years since that pioneering Guevarista-guerrilla experience in the mid-sixties – whose tradition left its imprint on later armed groups – a constellation of texts and images have portrayed period scenes in which revolutionary violence appears in vivid detail. In many testimonies, autobiographies and works of autofiction – including declarations prior to Jouvé's – there is the presence of the dreadful practice of summary justice that turns its weapons on the brother or sister suspected or accused of betrayal, weakness or lack of commitment. Despite this, the topic is surrounded by a form of discursive taboo. First, it reveals the blind obedience to a the higher command that violates ties of affection and friendship between fighters and equates them with enemies, a form of obedience marked by a warrior logic and a mystique of duty and hierarchy similar to that of the forces they were fighting against; and, second, such a practice offers another argument for equating the 'two' types of violence, that of the guerrilla group and that of illegal state repression (in Argentina, this attitude is epitomized in the 'theory of two demons' mentioned earlier), apportioning the guilt between the two 'bands' and contributing to a level of exoneration of those who administered death using state authority or its 'legitimate' repressive organs. This equating of deaths (the only difference being the merciless torture exercised by the repressors) leads to an affirmation of the cruelty, the 'inhumanity' of those who aspired to be defenders of a more just, more humane way of life.

Even though it can be roundly refuted by the definition of crimes against humanity established by the International

Criminal Court in The Hague in 1998, such equating continues in public discourse and in the ever elusive configuration of common sense.

Why then narrate these episodes? Why reveal the secret yet again, break the discursive taboo, allow that sordid history to see the light of day once more, revive those nightmarish scenes, speak again of the death sentences absurdly imposed on two named comrades of the same age and from the same background? One might consider it to be a narrative driven by repentance (somewhere between Bakhtin's 'confession' and a 'self-accounting'[5]) but without the necessity to confess in a trial or tribunal outside any form of condemnatory framework, almost for its own sake ... But it would perhaps be better to think of it as a debt never paid to one's own responsibility – although Jouvé did not personally kill anyone – a debt that continues as a command to others that is as valid as the 'never again'.

With all the importance and emotional impact that it supposes, after having suffered torture and imprisonment, taking up the threads of those events that also harboured grief at the deaths of other comrades from hunger or accident, it was not so much Jouvé's testimony that triggered the debate about the political violence of those years – and political violence *tout court* – as del Barco's letter. That letter focused on the theme of death and responsibility, his own – as, in his day, an ideological inspirer of that armed adventure – and that of all those who, in the name of the revolution, made a cult of death: 'serial killers', as he said, from 'Lenin, Trotsky, Stalin and Mao to Fidel Castro and Che Guevara',[6] not forgetting the leaders of the Argentinian guerrillas and their enemies, the generals of the dictatorship. Del Barco's 'call', as he himself defines it, sheltered by the banner of 'Thou shalt not kill', was not only a lament for the senseless deaths of those two very close beings in whom, with hindsight, he saw his own son, but it also introduced a radical proposition on ethics and responsibility that excluded mitigating circumstances and had no historical excuse; a proposition on the supremacy of the life of the Other which places an inalienable limit on all political action – an impossible but necessary principle, placed above any ideal, however noble, of social transformation.

The reaction to that letter was not long in appearing. Its impact overflowed the limits of words. Superficially, it divided the intellectual milieu into those who applauded the courage of del Barco's gesture, without completely agreeing with what he said, and those who considered it an insult or, worse still, a betrayal. The exchange was initially expressed in epistolary form,[7] with all the weight that genre has in terms of its unique articulation of the public and private, personal involvement – greater than in an essay or specialist article – and the fact of being written to be read both in solitude and as part of a media debate or a conversation, perhaps reworking that famous practice Habermas considered essential to the construction of modern public opinion: writing letters to be read by friends, in coffee houses, or published in newspapers, a practice that made the eighteenth century the *bildungsroman* century.[8]

The articulation between the public and private was, moreover, almost obligatory: the first responses came from the left – in its constitutive ambiguity and notorious diversity of nuances – and no one was excluded from the questions posed there: theoreticians, sympathizers, former militants, former *guerrilleros*, a heterogenic conglomeration but also a community of affinities. I do not specify the female gender here because it was, essentially – and typically, one might say, with a touch of malice – a masculine phenomenon. Despite the fact that many women were involved in the armed struggle and in militant organizations – not to mention their presence in the intellectual field – none joined the discursive showcase, or at least their voices were not included in the corpus of the first compilation.[9]

Public and private or, perhaps better, biographical, experience itself appeared as the unequivocal prop that authorizes the word. Each person responded to the challenge, thinking through – and evoking – his own biography: the events, the words spoken, the situations in which he participated, the losses, the sorrows, the opinions, shared or otherwise. An intimate tone unexpectedly surfaced, assertions were modulated by feeling: some voices spoke from a position of emotion and shock ('My friends, what have we been unable to hear?'; 'What strings has Oscar's letter set vibrating that we find them so mortifying?'[10]); others, basically those who decried the letter, spoke from the tedious exhaustion of their libraries or from an unrepentant 'confession'. Several responded by simply killing the messenger[11] or placed him in the enemy camp. What had been a 'call' – or as his friend Nicolás Casullo said, 'something beyond subjectivity, like an overflow of personal experience onto a plane that could be understood as the expiation of oneself and others'[12] – could not be heard as such by some. Instead, they read arguments. The aggressive tone continued *in crescendo* as 'counterarguments' began to appear, counterarguments that del Barco himself, in the second stage, set out to refute, this time in a discursive tone.

In summary, the letter was like a lightning bolt – or a thunderclap, according to Schmucler, resounding in the night like a force of nature: another way of knowing what is already known[13] – like a torch causing a fire, or an earthquake that shakes consciences. In Diego Tatián's opinion, it had a similar effect to Duchamp's found object: something impossible to accept in the context of (artistic) discourse. Something of the order of the unspeakable – or inaudible – possibly more like mumbling, quiet tones or intimate conversation, but which due to its dis-location, its untimely appearance, was paradoxically capable of producing an effect that no other modulated and contained reflection could have achieved. The 'Thou shalt not kill', Tatián continues, attempts to express 'what is impossible, inexpressible and inaccessible for a social-scientific vocabulary, journalistic phrasemaking or debates',[14] in the same way as the 'Bring them back alive' of human rights organizations succeeded in presenting the un-presentable, decanting a shared pain that could not be spoken in any other way.

If his detractors made supreme efforts to oppose the call, a level of surprise also arose among those close to him. Why bring that unbearable topic, that blind spot that once kept discussions between friends continuing into the night, into the public sphere? 'I confess, Oscar, that the passage into the visible of what had been whispered in private conversations, its enormous public and media presence, had a great impact on me.'[15] In this way, conversation and dialogue, preferably in private, appeared to be vying with debate as the most appropriate discursive genre for addressing a topic of such magnitude. Given the virulence of some of the responses, several participants – across a wide spectrum of Argentinian intellectuals – stressed the need for dialogic moderation, including in the public debate, a feature that would potentially help to confront the cause of the consternation with greater lucidity.

Of course, this was not the first time that the question of the 'appropriate genre' had arisen, particularly in relation to the traumatic experiences of Argentina's recent past. Is there a limit to what can be said in particular genres and, hence, to what can be heard? And does one say the same thing whatever the genre, or does each configure what is said, offer its own modulation, a different covering? The topic of the limits of representation, which was emblematic of reflection on the Holocaust,[16] to a great extent has to do with these questions of what could be called an ethics of genres; that is, the recognition and valorization, in usage, of the expressive – and performative – capacity that each genre has historically had to shape the word or image in accordance with certain thematic, compositional and stylistic norms – always susceptible to infraction – in the framework of a discursive formation. Testimony, auto/biography or the confession, for example, and even the novel, to the extent that it attempts to given an account of the lived experiences and sufferings of a community, carry an ethical promise that conforms to their systems of truth, the particular relationship they establish with their addressees, just as dialogue and conversation foster (without obligation) confidence, closeness and complicity.

That overlapping of genres had a more or less significant effect, depending on the various interventions: the epistolary, with its intimate and informal modulations; the essayistic, with its oscillation between the subjective and argumentative spheres; the testimonial, with its traumatic and/or accusatory mark; the autobiographical, marked by the legitimacy of experience ... All these genres brought something to a heteroclite discursive arena that at times became a battlefield.

But is there any way to contain the divergence of the various interpretations? Given such dilemmas, is it possible to find ways of understanding? The letter itself, its extreme (self-)accusation and regret, was only able to provoke such responses due to its excess of meaning. The debate – as some of his friends suggested – would not have taken place if it had been more restrained.

Because, in fact, the guerrilla activity, Che and Fidel's focalism, the exaltation of armed struggle and the cult of death on the part of the militants had all been thoroughly scrutinized, not only from the perspective of reformism or the journalistic construction of public opinion but even from sections of the left and Peronism (the 'national left') that had participated in different ways in the revolutionary project. During the dictatorship, these topics had been intensely discussed and reflected on both within Argentina and among those living in exile. One example is the magazine *Controversia*, published in Mexico by high-level militants from 1979 to 1981, which openly analysed the causes of the defeat and severely criticized methods that had cost the lives of so many militants and victims from 'the other side'. The contributions of Héctor Schmucler and Sergio Caletti, in particular, left no room for doubt in this respect. After the return to democracy, in accordance with the temporalities of memory mentioned earlier, after the proof of the repressive horror of state terrorism and its thousands of victims, after the (ongoing) recovery of the names and trajectories that the figure of disappearance attempted to erase, while the human remains and concentration camps were being uncovered, criminal prosecutions were being brought and stolen children sought, some of the topics of this debate began to emerge, if timidly, whether in fiction, testimony, intellectual opinion or academic research, producing in the last two decades a significant corpus of work.

However, both Jouvé's interview and del Barco's letter went further. Both of them foreground the protagonistic figure of the *I* with all its weight; that first person which confers on what it says the conclusiveness of explicit performativity, a distanced, testimonial *I* that does not evade its onerous, imprescriptible responsibility in the former case; an accusatory, critical and self-critical *I* in the latter, expressed through a desperate call in which emphasis and shock take precedence over the line of argument. That particular conjunction, produced in the ambit of philosophy, is a milestone in the politics of memory and in narratives of the recent past. It allows for an initial pulling aside of the veil of silence or the taboo of discourse, sufficient time having passed for addressing the grey area of the revolutionary elegy, the possibility of revisiting the cult of heroes without devaluing tributes to the victims or giving way to the temptation of concealing truths to avoid censure.

But if some effect was to be hoped for, the effects of meaning exceeded all expectations. True, the letter contained an essential ambivalence: the disarticulation of the public and private, the problematic coexistence of emotion and politics and the abruptness of the provocation. In terms of the line of argument, the letter was weak; in terms of the call, it was unbearable. Read literally, it was untenable.

Colophon

So was del Barco's call really heard? Or was it just a matter of silencing it immediately under a historical justification, the gloating of citations, philosophical or biblical sanctions? It was also a debate with a divine presence that could do honour to the title of Ernest Laclau's book *Misticismo, retórica y política* [*Mysticism, Rhetoric and Politics*].[17] There was, in fact, a great deal of that, as well as narcissism, exhibitionism and self-referencing. Some of those involved in the debate questioned del Barco's 'authenticity', as if that intangible, subjective term could invalidate the performative force of the word; others opined that the letter eclipsed the interview and thus undermined it. However, outside his circle of friends, voices in opposition joined the argument.

Those who heard that call bringing an ignominious act into the present – I include myself among them in a 'tenuous "we"', in Judith Butler's words[18] – possibly downplayed the harsher aspects of the letter that made its reading uncomfortable and focused on the power – and courage – of the gesture of both men: Jouvé's retelling – reliving – and del Barco's critical analysis of his own past.

As must be expected, the return to the past was shared by almost all of those who added their names to the argument. And in this weave of *I*s who looked below the surface of their own experience, there was a clear presence of one of the paradoxes of autobiography, that displaced temporality which gives pertinence to the question of who is speaking there. Who was that? The person he is today? The 'himself as other', as Ricoeur might say? The result of splitting – or the proof of the contingency of identity – that, in turn, requires complementary questions. For whom is this being spoken? Who is the recipient of the interlocution?

Some seemed to be speaking mostly about themselves in a form of interiority disturbed by painful memories. Others spoke from the pulpit or the platform. Yet others attempted to find new meanings for old questions, conscious of the risk of anachronism in relation to the past but unable to decide on the fairest evaluation of the present.

The point is that temporality always involves a problematic. How does one analyse, evaluate, those events located in a precise time and space imbued with the political logics and, in this case, unsullied beliefs of a youthful desire to 'change the world', with the mystique of revolution? Should it be from that past, with its justifications and norms, as if time had not elapsed? Or from today, from an updated critique of violence that involves a rejection of death whatever the situation, that form of ecology of life which comes to the fore – and takes on gigantic proportions – when life has increasingly less value? Or even from a species of 'in between', attempting to understand those logics but from a critical distance, taking on the weight of the past in the present, its *pendingness*, what it bequeaths us in terms of enlightening and dimming, what repeatedly filters into conversations, stories, into the decisions that might be taken in other, similar, circumstances?

That past, that sun 'rising in the sky of history', as Benjamin puts it,[19] comes out to meet us, irrupts into the word with the violence of remembrance or testimony to install a difference even in what is known: it was not the first time the awful details of Jouvé's story had been heard, but *this time* they had an effect that was almost a revelation. Some pointed out to del Barco that his reaction was excessive, given that he was already aware of the events. In his replies, he noted something that we perhaps all share in terms of experience: one does not know oneself en bloc, *all the time* – just as one does not remember all the time; one both knows and does not know oneself, particularly in the unfolding of trauma. And suddenly that knowing is brought into the present with all its ghostly horror and its unbearable turn: as

in 1995, for example, when the former naval officer Adolfo
Scilingo suddenly confessed on a television programme to
having *himself* been involved in the 'death flights' during the
dictatorship, when sleeping prisoners were thrown into the
sea ...[20]

But just as there are times for being able to speak, there
are also times for being able to *hear*. In some way, paradoxically, the letter foregrounded something in the order of
the *unspeakable*,[21] what is often removed from the debate,
discussion and criticism but in this case succeeded in being
the driving force behind them: it produced another form of
knowing, beyond the hero/martyr dilemma, a form of 'end
of innocence', as Vezzetti[22] points out, with respect to heroic
feats of the armed group.

From that knowledge which does not always speak everything about itself, from that past which persists without ever
crystallizing in the present, comes the question of whether
the legacy, the transmission of experience, is in fact possible.
In the ensemble cast of voices appears the hope that it is (in
Tatián, for instance), despite the intrinsic difficulty involved
in that transmission and the objections that can be raised to
the very concept of 'transmission'.

Due to the unusual coexistence of discursive genres, ranging
from the letter to the essay, the diatribe to introspection, the
first volume of *No matar* (*No Killing*) is an essential reference
in any consideration of the uneasy relationship between
the public and the private, between personal and collective
experience, singular or group memory(ies), and, hence, in
any consideration of the definition – construction – of public
memory, despite the urgent need for that definition, given
what continues to be a *recent* past.

Del Barco's letter, in which the voice of Levinas sounds
clearly (a voice that sounded again and again in the barbed
debate he carried on with his 'detractors' in the magazine
Conjetural and also in other exchanges), can be precisely
located in that clash – that bolt of lightning – of past and
present, like an explosion of 'existence', of 'life as it is lived';
that is to say, an ethics of responsibility, as Levinas claims,
that is not merely a theoretical posture but an unconditional
commitment to the other and to the life of the other (in
the sense of dying for that other) that involves the whole

of human behaviour, irrespective of avatars of History. In this vein, a clear similarity can be seen between Levinas and Bakhtin – both of whom recognize the influence of Martin Buber – in which the latter's dialogic concept of *answerability* involves not only giving an answer, a response, but also – and perhaps more importantly – responding for the Other; that is, accepting the other's pre-eminence in both discourse and life. So for that confession distanced in a chronicle, as Jouvé's interview can be read, there was a response from del Barco in terms of an ethical act, as Bakhtin[23] would term it, which, in assuming its own responsibility for the other, reaffirmed the intrinsic relationship between word (art) and life. This whole-hearted public involvement 'without protection, without reassurance', as his friend Héctor Schmucler wrote in a letter,[24] beyond the historicity of the event that had triggered it, moved towards a universality that many considered abstract and even imprudent. However, given the extreme fragility of life that seems to be our contemporary condition, given that indifference in the face of death that naturalizes the state of perpetual warfare, given that distinction between lives that 'deserve to be mourned'[25] and others that do not even have a name, del Barco's response did perhaps meet its tremendous challenge. And in doing so it opened up an unfathomable abyss, leaving us with a series of questions we may not be able to answer.

6
The Threshold, the Frontier: Explorations at the Limits[1]

Threshold, frontier, limit: signifiers that relentlessly stalk our everyday perceptions, what is permitted and prohibited, the decent and the reprehensible. But they also disrupt the incursion of language into the – now public – terrains of privacy and the hazardous transit between disciplines that traces out zones of uncertainty where nothing that is spoken is irrevocable. Artistic practices, writing and also the unfolding of the theoretical imagination all encourage an exploration of limits, in sync with contemporary life and the (supposed) evanescence of frontiers. Nevertheless, just as global connectivity offers the illusion of absolute ubiquity, these frontiers seem to be accentuated. Positioning myself on this edge that raises the – problematic – issue of 'inside' and 'outside', inclusion or exclusion – an ethical, aesthetic and public edge – I intend here to offer certain reflections on the practices and writings that work on frontier zones, defying or infringing the limits.

Language and transgression

Language, transgression and frontiers ... these are catch-words whose articulation is not immediately evident but which nevertheless mark out a recognizable spatiality that is physical, symbolic, territorial and subjective. It is an articulation that has, moreover, very sensitive connotations in Mexico, and that someone, not far from that land, worked admirably in the word, in language, in the body and in territory: Gloria Anzaldúa, a Chicana poet and writer whose emblematic text *Borderlands/La Frontera. The New Mestiza*,[2] written over twenty years ago, portrayed the troubled interior and exterior landscape of an unhappy northern frontier with the United States, asserting a new mestiza consciousness.

In this text, the cadences of the mother tongue, an essential component of what I shall provisionally call 'identity', acquire other modulations, take on new meanings, configure a space in constant disaccord with the territory – and a territory in disaccord with those Chicano inhabitants[3] – where translation and transgression come together and confront one another in an inevitable love–hate relationship: *Spanglish, Estandar English, North Mexican Spanish, Tex-Mex*? In the text, Anzaldúa undertakes an anthropological, poetic and political interrogation in which her own biography can be read in epic terms from collective, periodic, sometimes tragic gestures and from a historical setting that articulates such remote pasts as the mythic land of Aztlan, cradle of the pathways of Mesoamerica (hypothetically to be found underfoot) with a present of painful 'returns', all in the accents of everyday language, from the domestic imaginary, the tension between inherited tradition with its *deber-ser-mujer* (women's role) and her personal identity orientation/transgression: Chicana, lesbian, feminist, activist, poet ...

In this way, language, transgression and frontiers appear in almost obligatory conjunction, initiating a chain of semiosis that could well be defined, following Peirce, as infinite. The infinite webs of meaning which this conjunction is capable of triggering today in that territory, scarred by the infamous wall and the unceasing effort to cross it, even at risk of death,[4] is the case of other, different territories and other walls that, far from falling, continue to multiply in the second decade of the twenty-first century.

Here I see one of the many paradoxes of globalization: on the one hand it encourages ubiquity, unlimited connectivity in a virtual space that attempts to appear almost interstellar;

on the other, it exacerbates the partition of territories that renounces age-old traces and imposes impassable barriers on difference and inequality. Barriers that impede the polysemy of *frontier*: separation, threshold, door, contact, interchange and, why not, welcome, hospitality ... Because space is not a mere surface on which the gifts or inflictions of nature or the vestiges of cultures accumulate, but, as Doreen Massey states,[5] the constant (unfinished) product of intimate or global relationships and interactions and, hence, open to plurality and difference, to the march of time and history. Spatiality (space/temporality) is, then, political and gendered. It is of prime importance in the exercise – and division – of power, which faces the challenge of multiplicity, the complex mesh of interactions that go beyond frontiers; the enduring imaginary of mythologies; the identification of places as one's own (home, region, smallholding, town, village) in resistance to the stratification and ordering that divides the world into centres and peripheries (even when the periphery has moved to the centre or, hypothetically, they are all peripheries), into western and secondary languages, unstable or iron barriers; or both at once, depending on which side you try to pass, as in the militarized San Diego–Tijuana border, a hotspot of that tragic 'northern frontier'.[6]

An obsessive partition – and redistribution – of territory, with the addition of new frontiers inserted where none had been before, invasions, trafficking, pillaging, the expulsion of whole populations, fear-fuelled migrations, harassment or poverty; the exploitation of areas rich in natural resources without thought for those living there: all these factors make territoriality a decisive element in this stage of capitalism. A capitalism which seems to be constantly shifting further from its 'metaphysical' nature, as Scott Lash[7] defines it, referring to the division of power consummated on the liquid-crystal displays of global stock exchanges without the presence of any material authority. Or it can be imagined that the virtual also inevitably looms over those territories and that the perpetual warfare that destroys distant lands is its model and its price.

But internal frontiers between populations that might justify belonging to a place are also more sharply defined: urban frontiers marked out by the process of gentrification, with the consequent emptying out of areas in decline to make way for populations, or the progressive marginalization of certain neighbourhoods while others are transformed following trends in design and fashion.[8]

Unstable frontiers that become iron in given circumstances can be dangerous for unnoticed passers-by or leave room for the emergence of ghettos so perilous that one needs (linguistic or visual) safe conduct to traverse them, as is the case with the so-(badly)called 'urban tribes', whose identity recognition is also territorial. And there are also gated communities that attempt to construct a barrier between themselves and an ill-defined, disturbing 'outside'. Whatever the case, the imposition of a boundary, a frontier, carries the threat of and desire for transgression.

The fact is that transgression is contained in the very notion of the frontier, as in the simple exercise of language; it could even be said that it is the secret force behind every transit. From the forced eternal return of those who try again and again to cross 'from the other side', where the difficulty of access seems to increase the fantasy, to the signifiers that guide our daily perception. Threshold, frontier, limit all signal, for example and possibly *in crescendo*, the level of the incursion of language into territories of intimacy, a level that likewise could – beyond the classic modern distinction between public and private – be expressed in the subtle ascent involved in passing from the (perfectly public) biographical to the (not so perfect) private and intimate, which today forms the greatest attraction of the media, an intimacy become public, in a generalized transgression, and so stereotypical.

So what can be truly considered transgressive in contemporary societies where, in contrast to what happens in physical territories, there is a growing blurring of limits and frontiers that in general terms can only be welcomed? Greater conceptual openness, a weakening of the norm, a culture-world, as some authors like to call it,[9] stimulated not only by technology but also by travel and voluntary migration, all strongly influence the processes of the formation of subjectivity and identity reconfiguration, both at individual and collective levels, generating a – for some, disturbing – liminality between what were once relatively autonomous practices and spaces.

Such practices of everyday life are, of course, largely fed by global connectivity and its imposition of forms, habits and modes of life; academic and intellectual spaces in which an irreverent attitude to established canons has encouraged transdisciplinary approaches; artistic practices that set aside questions about the work to develop their formal and conceptual communicability in the pressing context of the present; practices of writing which have so little respect for canons that they become unclassifiable – or post-autonomous, as Josefina Ludmer defines them.[10]

Permeability is also shown in the positive consideration of interstitial spaces, as expressed by the theoretical figures of the *interval* and the *in between* ('border zones' of thought as Bakhtin, ahead of his time, put it, that unfold at the 'junctures and points of intersection' of disciplines[11]) and in the evaluation of ambiguity, the unsayable, what could be one thing or its opposite, a recurrent theme within deconstruction.

In these developments, the expression of subjectivity, the voice and presence, occupy a privileged position. Transgressing their canonical spaces, narratives of the *I* – and their many masks – blur into a wide variety of genres and registers of culture (auto/biographical, testimonial, memorial, autofictional) and offer the gift of 'real' experience. Here too ethical and aesthetic limits have been crossed and new modulations appear in the incessant buzz of social discourse, in writing, on screens – all forms of them – on stages, in museums and the like, in public art and street performance, narratives whose diversity defies any attempt at taxonomy and, perhaps for that reason, are the ideal environments for bearing witness to present-day transformations of subjectivity, identities, memory and individual and collective experience. It is their *mise en forme*, their 'putting in meaning', that allows the analytical articulation of their ethical, aesthetic and political dimensions.

In that 'bearing witness' to the event, in that *mise en forme*, the image – in the culture of the image – undoubtedly plays a leading role. The moving image, in its innumerable registers: from documentary to video art, from the institutional to the domestic and marginal spheres; the still photograph where, despite technological manipulation, art has recovered its aura of verisimilitude – perhaps due to the responsibility it has

shouldered for revealing the monstrous face of the world –
as it comes to the fore in artistic practices with its powerful
metaphorical impact.

Art on the frontier

It was precisely through the image that the frontier (that
frontier which Gloria Anzaldúa draws with the iconicity of
the word and the performative power of language, straining
the limits between translation and transgression) returned
like an urgent questioning in response to the Catalan
artist Antoni Muntadas's 2005 artwork *On Translation/
Fear/Miedo*, dealing with the San Diego–Tijuana border,
which formed part of *La Memoria del Otro* (*The Memory
of the Other*),[12] a video art exhibition curated by Anna
María Guasch in the Museo Nacional de Bellas Artes in
Santiago, Chile in 2010. This piece brings together works
that translate a common concern of diverse regions of the
planet: how to give voice and presence – from an aesthetico-
critical perspective – to endangered ways of life, landlessness,
migration, humiliation, uprooting, the diaspora. That 'how'
needed a particular type of artist whom Guasch described in
these terms:

> That 'other artist' is someone interested in a social – not class
> but territorial – discourse, not so much a creator of images as
> a researcher of them, who brings together, creates, questions,
> recounts and exhibits iconic or other information on universal
> topics ... in order to unmask, uncover, denounce, analyse ...
> censored, humiliated, or violated aspects of the modern world.[13]

Muntadas's work, which integrates a series of pieces under
the title *On Translation*, had been created for an event
organized by inSite 05, a contemporary art project based in
the bi-national Tijuana–San Diego region, funded by both
the United States and Mexico and dedicated to commis-
sioning and promoting new work in the public domain.[14]
The artist's aim was for the 30-minute video to be projected
on both sides of the border and shown on public television
in two centres of power (Mexico City and Washington, DC)

in order to intervene in one area of the media that exercises the greatest control and influence in the communication era.[15]

Bearing witness, once again, to the 'narrative turn' of contemporary public art,[16] the Catalan artist also chose to start from language, creating a tension between translation and humankind's most common feeling, *Fear/Miedo*, an experience shared on both sides of the frontier, each in its own way: in San Diego, fear of the arrival of narco-trafficking, of cheap, undocumented labour, of a language whose expansion threatens English; in Tijuana, wedded to hope, a more physical fear of being caught by *la migra* (the immigration police; ICE), of deportation, of losing one's life or leading a precarious existence without the luxury of permanent residency. The language of art distances itself here from such hackneyed signifiers as violence and victimization – and, thus, compassion – to give the voice, on both sides in both languages, to interviewees of different ages, sexes, social classes and ideological positions in an audio-visual collage of texts, statistics, views of the landscape intersected by the menacing line of the wall, film images – some memorable – advertisements, news bulletins, music ... The socio-anthropological distance of an aesthetic gaze that operates, in the spirit of Bakhtinian dialogism, by bringing together – and, thus, opening the possibility of the response – the respective prejudices and deep ignorance of the *other*, knowingly fed by governments, the media and the trafficking, that 'industry of fear', as the artist puts it, which flourishes in and thanks to the frontier, a web of negotiations that defies any dichotomous interpretation to the benefit of some and the detriment of others. The frontier, he seems to tell us, beyond its function as a physical barrier, is established as symbolically and symbiotically *invisible to both sides*, and the challenge of fear – and also its victims – is played out in the in-between, a 'between' place which, I would venture to say, those who cross 'from the other side' will never leave behind: it will always be another junction between languages and cultures in translation, with its gains and losses, its unspeakable 'neither ... nor'. It is a place that we possibly share without having crossed a physical frontier to settle, that could be defined, metonymically, as a way of being contemporary.

> On Translation is a series
> of works that explore
> questions of transcription,
> interpretation and translation.
>   From language to codes
>   From silence to technology
>   From subjectivity to objectivity
>   From agreement to wars
>   From private to public
>   From semiology to cryptography
> The role of translation /
> translators as a fact,
> visible / invisible.[17]

But Muntadas did not only deal with the 'northern frontier' in the Santiago de Chile exhibition; he also included the parallel work *On Translation/Miedo/Jauf*,[18] which addresses the Tarifa (Spain)–Tangier (Morocco) marine frontier with its *pateras*,[19] with the fear of being shipwrecked and terrorism as other essential components. The artist Krzysztof Wodiczko[20] also exhibited, among other works, *The Tijuana Projection*, a performative intervention made for inSite 02, which was projected onto the facade of the Omnimax Theatre in the Centro Cultural de Tijuana (CECUT: popularly known as 'la Bola' [the Ball] due to its spherical shape), a building conceived with the aims of revitalization and integration: Tijuana as a tourist and cultural attraction, not simply the realm of narco-trafficking, prostitution and what might be called 'the high life'.

On this occasion the artist, who often works with large-scale transgressions that project voiced images onto emblematic buildings or places to establish a subversive and critical connection with them (as is the case with *The Hiroshima Projection*,[21] also included in the exhibition), projected the greatly enlarged faces of female workers from Tijuana-bonded assembly plants onto the building, offering real-time narratives of their working and family lives, the effects of their work on their health, sexual abuse, family breakdowns, alcoholism, domestic and political violence, so expressing the dislocation of their lives in Tijuana (also an internal frontier in its own country) in contrast to the space of integration which the CECUT represents.

Tijuana. It's a border not only between Mexico and the United States, but also between Tijuana and the rest of Mexico ... for many people who come from poor provinces such as Chiapas to try to advance their life by moving north. They cross the border before they reach Tijuana. That's the border between the feudal village and work in the maquiladora factory as members of a new kind of industrial proletariat. They say they move from an old hell to a new hell. For many of them, that's an advantage. Perhaps there is nothing worse than to stay in the same hell all their life long.[22]

On that 'facade' – perhaps accentuating the usage of the word as mere appearance – faces, voices and stories, biographical moorings of collective suffering (short stories, memories, dreams, small scenes that, in public, generated a strange intimacy) defied the abstract monumentalism and silence, showing what is unspoken, everyday poverty, the real effects of that peculiar chronotope (fear, the frontier) on modes of coexistence, self-recognition, identities and spiritual life. In this way, the intervention transformed a hi-tech spectacle capable of attracting audiences, real presences in real places, into a critical art experience.[23]

But exactly what is critical art? According to Chantal Mouffe, it is 'art that foments dissensus, that makes visible what the dominant consensus tends to obscure and obliterate'.[24] With that 'makes visible', Mouffe is drawing a broad distinction between two tendencies related to theoretical or political orientation: the involvement in a counter-hegemonic conflict in *the interior* of institutions, utilizing their media and technologies to challenge and subvert canons and norms (an attitude that coincides with her own definition of the political in terms of *agonism*; the struggle for hegemony[25]) or rather the 'exodus' from existing institutions in the conviction that desertion is the only form of resistance at this stage of capitalism.[26]

The works of both Muntadas and Wodiczko are, in their different ways, inscribed in the first of these tendencies. The two artists work on similar genres of entertainment and the communications media, altering their logics, demonstrating the potentiality of the transgression of the languages employed, their repetition and stereotyping. Beyond its aesthetic execution, *Fear/Miedo* sets up a dialogue between languages and perceptions that are constantly crossing the frontier in a mode rarely used by news programmes or interviews, which tend to offer radically conflicting positions or support one of those conflicting attitudes. *The Tijuana Projection*, for its part, gives a 'space of appearance' – in Arendt's sense of appearance as a fundamental aspect of the democratic public sphere[27] – for voices and faces to speak what is more commonly found in the political pages of newspapers or heard in the murmur of conversation than through the biographical accounts of the actors themselves. Moreover, the appearance of the disturbingly large face and the referential adaptation could be interpreted as the ethical sense Levinas conferred on the sight of the face of the other; not as the perception of its details, but what is irreducibly human in it: '[T]here is an essential poverty in the face. The face is exposed, menaced, as if inviting us to an act of violence. At the same time, the face is what forbids us to kill.'[28]

In both works there is a *mise en scene* – outside the conventional 'scene' – that is attentive to the feelings involved (their affections), confers visibility and takes on the dramatic tension of confrontation while rejecting sentimentality and media banality. Here also allusion, elision, the fragmentary nature of memory and the hesitancy of narration are explicit, with no attempt at explanation, closure or conclusion.

In a web of coincidence, in 2010, at the Tate Modern, London, I visited a retrospective of the work of Francis Alÿs, a Belgian artist who lives and works in Mexico City but has carried out projects in distant countries. Two of his works in particular highlight heart-rending aspects of the frontier: *The Green Line* and *The Loop*.[29] The first was a video of a performance that consisted of the artist leaving a trail of green paint while walking along the hypothetical 1948 line dividing Israel and Jordan; after the Six Day War (1967), Israel moved east to seize the Palestinian West Bank and the Gaza Strip to the west of the line. Traversing streets, walls, wasteland, before the astonished or indignant eyes of passers-by, the artist aimed to restore a living memory of the green line that had been drawn between the two states on the original map, marking his protest against the present territorial demarcation and the despicable wall being erected as he passed. *The Loop* again refers to the paradigmatic Tijuana–San Diego frontier in an unusual procedure, travelling half the world so as to avoid crossing it. As another participant in inSite (1997), Alÿs decided that rather than make an on-site work, he would use his fee to draw a physical, territorial arc (the loop); starting from Tijuana, he travelled down the coast to Santiago de Chile, crossed the Pacific to New Zealand, then continued to Australia, Singapore, Hong Kong and the whole of the contour of East Asia, before going on to Alaska, Canada and the United States, finally arriving in San Diego six weeks after he set out, without once having crossed a frontier. The performance takes on physical form in a postcard with a marine view, on the back of which is a map showing his route. The artist distributed the postcard at every stage of his journey and it was available to the public in the gallery. Under the piece was the following inscription:

> In order to go from Tijuana to San Diego without crossing the Mexico–United States border, I followed a perpendicular route away from the fence and circumnavigated the globe heading 67° South East, North East and South East again until I reached my departure point. The project remained free and clear of all critical implications beyond the physical displacement of the artist.[30]

The work had a twofold objective: on the one hand, to lay critical stress on the intrinsic difficulties and hardships involved in crossing that frontier; on the other, it offers an ironic comment on the performance itself and the excesses of art-world travel in the nineties. It is also interesting to consider the duplicity of both aesthetic options, which carry out the critical act as allegory and literality: the line on the map traced on the earth, on territory, as memory of the accord infringed by war and annexation; digression as a method – as was mentioned in the first chapters of this book – is shown here in physical and territorial displacement. In both cases, the artist operates more as the medium of the action than a true protagonist.

Another critical modality, ritual and commemorative in nature, dealing with those who lost their lives crossing the frontier, was shown in *La Nube/The Cloud*, an intervention

by the Chilean artist Alfredo Jaar, who also participated in
inSite in 2000. Jaar carried out a performance he defined as
an 'ephemeral monument' in a canyon on the border, close
to Playas de Tijuana, in the presence of, among others, the
families of the victims. The work consisted of the release
of three thousand white balloons contained in a net shaped
like a cloud, representing the souls of the men, women and
children who had succumbed to the gunfire of border patrols,
pursuit or the extreme climate in their attempt to reach the
Promised Land. The action took place on the Mexican side
of the border, near the wall on a sunny day under a clear
blue sky, and the release was accompanied by recitations and
music by Bach and Albinoni, performed by instrumentalists
on the Mexican side and a soloist on the United States side
(where there was no audience).

> *The Cloud* lasted 45 minutes in which we offered a space and
> time of mourning. Music was played on both sides of the border,
> symbolically uniting a divided land and people. Poetry was
> read and a moment of silence was observed. Then the balloons
> were released. Contrary to normal wind conditions, the wind
> that morning took an unexpected turn and pushed the balloons
> towards Mexico. Catalina Enriquez, Felix Zavala, Guadalupe
> Romero, Trinidad Santiago, Aureliano Cabrera and the others
> went back home.[31]

As in other works by Jaar, this piece shows a desire to bear
witness to the atrocity of *number* – in relation to the victims
– where the names spoken attempt to recover the quality
of *person*, and also its difficulty, the necessary distance of
the representation, which once again takes an indirect and
allegorical form.

Public art/critical art

In their different ways, each of these interventions by internationally recognized artists brought together locality – and
its hotspot, the frontier – the global scene and the geopo-
litical, economic, ethnic and cultural tensions of this stage
of capitalism, bearing witness, perhaps inadvertently, to that

slightly enigmatic signifier, 'the global'. Moreover, each one, in its style, affirms the potential of critical art for *creating* public space and not merely happening in it. Because, as Rosalyn Deutsche states:

> Discourse on public art tends to assume that art is public if it is located in physical spaces outside museums or galleries, such as urban squares. On automatically accepting that such spaces are public, the discourse on public art conceals the fact that they are, like any other social space, subject to restrictions, dominated by private economic interests and controlled by the state, under the aegis of urban planning. On assuming that spaces outside art institutions are public, art is given affirmative and decorative roles, and that is so deeply embedded in the discourse on public art as to make the term meaningless in critical terms. From my viewpoint, the public condition of a work of art is not rooted in its location in a space defined as public, but in the fact that it carries out an operation: *the operation of making space public by transforming any space that the work occupies into what can be called a public sphere.* (My italics).[32]

In conjunction with that statement, my chance encounter – and that of many other people – with these works was not 'live', in the 'presence' of the event that took place *on or near* the frontier, but occurred in their posterity, in their almost obligatory development as exhibits in high-status institutions within the canonical model of the exhibition or retrospective. But that public space of critical art also has a role (although fragmentarily, and without the impact of the presence of the moment and place) on the Web, in the possibility of following, within given limitations, the careers of the artists discussed here and their 'bypasses', to borrow an expression used by Alÿs, that take them ever more frequently to distant corners of the planet.[33] And it also allows us, when we write about them, to shed the guilt of not showing the images.

This notion of critical public art is compatible with Chantal Mouffe's in her emphasis on the political aspects of art: 'What makes all of these very diverse artistic practices critical ones [she gives the examples Barbara Kruger, Hans Haacke, Wodiczko, etc.] is that, albeit in different ways, they can be seen as *agonistic interventions* in the public space'[34] (my italics).

Returning to the public space of the frontier, as one of the conclusions to his study of a period of the inSite contemporary art programme, García Canclini[35] points out that both anthropology and artistic practices have greater resources for perceiving the nuances of the problematic of frontiers in terms of situations that separate but also communicate. In fact (beyond the real intercultural nature of the bi-national region of San Diego/Tijuana, the mixture of languages, food and customs, the rituals that have always crossed the frontier, the millions who make a living 'from the other side' and those who pass 'from this side' for tourism, shopping or business), the menacing barrier, constructed from metal sheets the United States forces had used to form landing strips in the desert during the Gulf War – a not insignificant form of recycling – that supports the everyday activity of those who come and go in the bustle of street vendors[36] is to some extent porous and, despite the intimidating paraphernalia of watchtowers, metal fencing, cameras and patrols, has leaks (children who pass to play 'on the other side') and encourages the transit of those who attempt to cross it, knowing that they are not wanted. Something of this multifaceted reality and the subjectivities it generates can be seen in the video art of Muntadas, who, in contrast to the other artists mentioned here, worked on both sides, using a montage of images to show a dialogic movement – without any sense of consensus – that would have been difficult to produce in real life, leaving the signifying chain open, far from a manifesto or 'victimology', but with a clear agonistic intention.[37]

> One of the things that resulted from *Fear/Miedo* was that after the people who had collaborated on the project viewed it, one of them asked me for a copy to show to the border patrol police, because he thought they should see and hear the opinions coming from Tijuana and San Diego, opinions that are the product of the fear generated by situations they are partly responsible for, but never heard. It seems like that work is defining a public that it might have some effect on. Fantastic, but that doesn't always happen.[38]

So, why have I included these 'explorations at the limits' here?

My first response is perhaps slightly personal: a passion for the visual that coexists with a passion for language. Second, and more concretely, I believe that it is interesting to reflect on these forms of articulating the spheres of theory, aesthetics, ethics and politics from a 'critical subjectivity' or a perception that 'requires involvement', as Muntadas proposes[39]; or, as Alÿs says of *The Green Line*, 'Sometimes doing something poetic can become political and sometimes something political can become poetic.'[40] These are indirect, metaphorical, allegorical forms that also address the very conception of transdisciplinarity as the imaginary inter-section of different knowledges, crossovers, passages between different fields, simultaneous, multiple visions of an object of study in relation to a *now*,[41] disdaining the patrolling of frontiers – disciplines – so dear to certain positions even now in the first decades of a new century. Of course, this does not involve any sense of lightness or improvisation; it is rather an openness, a hearing, a disposition towards the other (the other knowledge, the other gaze, simply the Other). Daring to move out from the enclosure that specialization at times involves – without devaluing it – towards *spatiality*, it could be said, towards what diverse narratives (philosophy, cinema, the arts, literature, poetry) have to say about our conflictive present.

In the same way, the threshold and the frontier delineate a symbolic place for ethics in the construction of the self and other, where fear, discrimination and violence can flourish and reinforce stereotypical prejudices. Here also is the terrain of the exploration at the limits – of power, knowledge, authority – where voices, memories and biographies are essential for the recognition, both in terms of the personal and of shared, lived experiences.

Finally, with a nod to Peirce's semiotic triad, there is a third possible response to the reason for this exploration that has led me, through chance journeys and those coincidences that are not really coincidental, to find – choose – these works and these artists: *biographical space*, a topic I have already explored in some detail but never before from a personal perspective: the fortuitous fact of having a son who lives in San Diego and perceiving, on each visit, from a distant gaze (from the Spanish of Buenos Aires, from our mythical frontier at the 'end of the world') the contradictions and tensions, the particular symbiosis of that 'two-sided' region, the unequal struggle of languages and cultures and the menacing line of the frontier, although my Argentinian passport excuses me from fear.

7

The Name, the Number

The number, in the atrocious dimension of the tally of victims, accompanies our daily lives with astonishing naturalness. In the unsleeping flow of news on screens, figures pile up day after day: distant war scenes, the focuses of which flare up time after time, bombings, confrontations, catastrophes, exoduses, massacres. The number is variable and we no longer know how much is *a lot*; or if the deaths can be measured arithmetically. Nothing is new, of course, and the present state of violence seems to establish itself above greater horrors from the past: the First World War, the Armenian genocide, the 'final solution', Hiroshima, Latin American dictatorships and, only yesterday, Rwanda ... We do know, however, that we are not safe; that no form of rationality can erase the mark of the past; that renewed state now 'global' violence comes into play[1]; that although there is talk of 'humanitarian wars', the bombs will fall on civilian populations and the fateful number will continue to predominate – at the expense of names – in stark news reports, once again bearing witness to 'horrorism'.[2]

This state of the world is also translated into images that challenge the tolerance of the gaze and constantly pose the age-old dilemma of representation: what to show and how to show it, whether it be in the well-known press photograph (which has its moment of glory in international exhibitions), artistic practice (the two are at times notoriously close) or in what the word manages to *make seen* through its own metaphorical potential.

Throughout the chapters of this book, the violence of the number – and the survival of the name – are evoked with symptomatic insistence in the images and words that outline a shared zone: in the memorial mark of the war and the Shoah that persists in Sebald and Boltanski; in the traumatic experience of the Argentinian dictatorship through the voices of women; in the debate of intellectuals and former militants; in Jaar's and Wodiczko's artistic practices related to the space of the frontier and also, like an Aleph that contains and refracts a large part of my journeys, in the work of those artists in other massacre scenes (Rwanda, Hiroshima) that I include under the section heading 'Naming'. It was not initially thought of as a thematic line to be developed through the work of the authors and artists brought together here, and the a posteriori confirmation came to bear witness not only to a possible retrospective effect of the writing but also to the profound harmony between the voices and emotions set in dialogue here. The title of this chapter came after writing the text as undeniable proof involving a level of Borgesian reminiscence – although his numbers occupy a superior order of a different and distant mathematics to the one which (pre)occupies me here in a terrifying, inaccessible infinity.

On the massacre

In chapter 1, 'The Gaze as Autobiography: Time, Place, Objects', I included a quotation in which Sebald assumes the voice of Thomas Browne to unfold a dazzling metaphor related to massacre and the periodic number of its occurrences, occurrences that seem to happen as naturally as the sun sets. The metaphor has that mythic tone which in some way tinges *The Rings of Saturn* with melancholy and for me brought to mind an article in which the art historian Gastón Burucúa refers to the problem of the representation of massacre since ancient times and offers an interesting reflection that is highly pertinent to the cases that will be discussed later:

What the Greeks perceived is that massacre, being dispossessed of all legitimacy, cannot be included in a logical series of events. Violence, killing, war can be understood. But massacre cannot be explained. What exists, then, is a radical disparity between the perpetrator and the victim. The victim is defenceless, at a disadvantage and incapable of reacting. That disparity is what defines massacre. The victim cannot resist, cannot respond. So, the difficulty of representation has to do with the impossibility of explaining it rationally.[3]

That difficulty of representation can be clearly perceived in *On the Natural History of Destruction*,[4] where massacre acquires the real, historical form of the bombing of the civilian populations of German cities, a topic that is occluded, taboo, not only in Germany. Sebald lingers on an obsessive tally of tons of bombs, their characteristics and effects, the number of bombardments and mortality figures and, in a form of memorial tribute – in the face of the lack of representation – revives the few voices that tell something of what happened in scenes of unimaginable horror. At the end of the chapter, I suggest a certain unexpected correspondence with Boltanski, who has also faced the dilemma of the representation of the Shoah, this time in his artistic practice, where his aesthetic *parti pris* for suggesting the uncountable number of victims is translated into piles of clothing, establishing a metonymic, deeply disturbing relationship with the body/bodies. The same is true of his work on photographs: faces – still without names – that attempt to restore the ethical circuit of the gaze, recognition and pain, possibly posing the question, as does Mitchell,[5] of what images *really want* (of us), beyond anguish and compassion.

In chapter 3, 'Memory and Image', the number also looms over Austerlitz's compulsive journeying through the train stations of Europe in search of the truth about the past, spurred by the mystery surrounding his origins, a number that has definitely assaulted my perception of travellers when taking a train, on some occasion, and travelling even a short distance over that cartography forever marked by tragedy. By contrast, returning to the chapter, the sudden discovery in Liverpool Street station revealed that other trains *had carried* Jewish children, like Austerlitz, to save them from the most awful of deaths. My two characters – Sebald and Boltanski – again coincide in an image from *Storage Area of the Children's Museum*,[6] one room of which the artist donated to the Musée d'Art Moderne de la Ville de Paris.

The distance of the number

In the experience of the last Argentinian dictatorship, the atrocity of the number is wedded to the perverse figure of disappearance: the disappearance of bodies and names, of remains and the traces, that leaves a deep open wound, not only in the family but also in the civic and social weaves since the loss cannot be completely assumed in any of these cases – not even in the cold statistics of the state apparatus – and neither can it be honoured with the appropriate rites of death and mourning. But in chapter 4, 'Women Who Narrate', the relationship between name and number has another meaning, also linked to dispossession: the replacement of the former by the latter; that is to say, the erasure of the person, biography and individuality through the most famous of concentration camp practices: divesting the victim of her humanity. In both Calveiro's *Poder y desaparición (Power and Disappearance)*[7] and the *Conversations of Five Women Survivors*,[8] the problematic of the number imposed in the camp appears in the narrative development of trauma and is possibly one of the aspects that drive the will to *authority/authorship* in the present, speaking from the name and so justifying agency and the public declaration of personal identity. However, in the interlinked threads of their conversations, the five women did not feel particularly affected by having to respond to a number: rather, they experienced it as a wall protecting their own intimacy, given the strange conditions that formed part of their captivity, among which was being available to accompany their captors on excursions outside, in the city.[9]

Ethics and responsibility

In the 'del Barco debate', which I dealt with in chapter 5, the extreme violence exercised by a guerrilla group on its own

comrades in the early sixties – which would leave its mark
on the modes of action of the armed groups of the following
decade – becomes the focus of a heated epistolary polemic
involving intellectuals, psychoanalysts, journalists and former
militants which was later compiled in a book. The trigger of
this debate, as has been said, was a letter written by Oscar
del Barco, published in the magazine *La Intemperie*, entitled
'No matarás' ('Thou Shalt Not Kill'), in response to the events
that a survivor of the group, Héctor Jouvé, described in an
interview published in the same media organ.[10] As was seen,
the positions that developed in the letters, published over
two years or more in *La Intemperie* and other magazines
and internet sites, could be broadly grouped into: those who
emphasized a conception of ethics viewed (self-)critically from
the present, where the end, however just it might be, does not
justify the means; those whose reading of the events exalted
the ideals at play at that point in history; and those who
considered that neither the question of ethics nor the potential
of a revolutionary ideal could be avoided. The debate – still
ongoing – is silhouetted against the horrors of Nazism and
war, the violence of state terrorism and the violence of Latin
American revolutionaries, discussions in which philosophical,
religious, ideological and political arguments are deployed
and in which the number fluctuates between the fateful thirty
thousand (of disappeareds) and two particular cases – the ones
that initiated the polemic – in which it is the *name* (and not
the number) that awakens a memory and that carries with it
an awful burden.

> As I read Jouvé's succinct and clear account of the murder
> of Adolfo Rotblat (whom they called Pupi) and Bernardo
> Groswald, I felt as though they had killed my own son, and
> the person who was asking why, how and where was me. At
> that moment, I realized clearly that because I had supported
> the actions of that group I was as responsible as those who
> had killed him. But it wasn't just a question of me assuming
> responsibility in general but of assuming responsibility for the
> murder of two human beings with names: all of the group
> and all those of us who supported it in whatever way, either
> inside or outside, are responsible for the murder of Pupi and
> Bernardo.[11]

In that declaration of responsibility, del Barco is in complete accord with Levinas's ethic, which was also at play in the debate. In Levinas's own words:

> My responsibility is untransferable, no one could replace me. In fact, it is a matter of saying the very identity of the human I starting from responsibility ... Responsibility is what is incumbent on me exclusively, and what, humanly, I cannot refuse. This charge is a supreme dignity of the unique. I am I in the measure that I am responsible, a non-interchangeable I.[12]

Naming

The name and the number have a particular relevance in the work of the artists Krysztof Wodiczko (*The Hiroshima Projection*)[13] and Alfredo Jaar (*The Rwanda Project*),[14] both of whom participated in the inSite experiences mentioned in chapter 6 and whose practices can be defined as a critical art that privileges public space for the achievement of their aims.

As was mentioned in that chapter, during the preparation of *The Hiroshima Projection*, Wodiczko carried out cross-generational interviews with survivors and descendants who had suffered the physical and psychological consequences of the nuclear attack; he recorded the testimonies on tape and videoed the hands of the speakers. The work consisted of a large-scale projection onto water (the river that runs through the Hiroshima Memorial Park) of the expressive hands that accompanied the voices of the testimonies, with the emblematic backdrop of the Atomic Bomb Dome, parts of which were still standing after the bomb was dropped and which is lit differently each night. For two nights (6 and 7 August) on the anniversary, thousands of people attended the projection, which in some way defied the official tendency to silence the traumatic story and memory. The idea of this 'commemoration therapy' was not only to give voice to those protagonists but also to symbolically invest the old ruined building with a new expressive capacity. In this way, the dialogue between the water (a shroud for those who threw themselves into it, believing it would soothe their wounds), the hands, the voices and the almost protective backdrop of the Dome produced an effect of high-density significiation (the stories both translate past suffering and carry issues of discrimination, prejudice, racism and intolerance into the present), plus originality in terms of the mode of representation.[15]

Among the most outstanding of the testimonies is that of a woman called Kwak Bok Soon, who tells of a visit she made to the United States Department of State as part of a delegation of survivors who hoped to hand in a petition against the nuclear tests. In this account, the number takes on a chilling presence.

> I recall an official of the Department, who was very young and handsome, came out. As one of the victims of the bomb, Mr. Hasegawa appealed to him with all his heart to stop the tests. Otherwise, the Earth would be ruined and all humanity would be destroyed. Then the official started discussing the theory of nuclear deterrence. I could tolerate his theory up to a certain point. But he said something at the end. He said that dropping the bomb was absolutely not wrong. He said that it was thanks to that the war could be ended earlier and at least the lives of 200,000 soldiers were saved... . When I heard the official's voice saying 200,000 lives, my hair bristled with anger, and I remembered that the bomb took 200,000 lives in a single moment when Hiroshima was bombed ... 'Excuse me? Who do you think you're saying this to? ... People who suffered because of the bomb have come to talk to you eagerly about wanting to save the Earth, when they could instead be blaming you for the lives you impaired.' I felt that way, at that time. And I didn't have the words to protest to him then. In fact, I didn't say a single word. All I did there was cry my heart out. I couldn't do anything other cry ... I tried to say something. In my mind I was shouting, 'How dare you throw such things out at people who are victims!' I truly wished I could have yelled, 'What the devil are you thinking?' But I wasn't able to put it in words, and I left the Department sobbing. When I returned to Japan, I joined the meeting in which we reported our experiences and actions as victims, and I spoke of my experiences for the first time. Really, I hated talking. I absolutely didn't want to talk... . but now I think this way: People who died, died without speaking [a word]. I survived and am alive, on their behalf, so I must dare to talk without feeling embarrassed about hating it. I am talking about it now, knowing that it is my mission.[16]

In an analysis of the precariousness of contemporary life, Judith Butler refers to the differentiation that operates at every level, even in terms of the value given to human life, which should be an absolute. What in fact happens is that '[c]ertain lives will be highly protected, and the abrogation of their claims to sanctity will be sufficient to mobilize the forces of war. Other lives will not find such fast and furious support and will not even qualify as "grievable"'.[17] The response that so deeply wounded Kwak Bok Soon is precisely expressed in that difference, that radical disparity of the gaze where the other does not attain the status of human.

In relation to the Chilean artist Alfredo Jaar, his work addresses a broad thematic spectrum in which concerns about Africa and other war-torn regions predominate. His *Rwanda Project*,[18] in particular, includes several emblematic works that have left a deep impression on contemporary art criticism. The 1994 genocide of the Tutsi minority carried out by the Hutu tribe, which, in the face of the indifference of the government and international bodies, left a total of a million dead in one hundred days, led Jaar to travel to Rwanda in August of that year to see with his own eyes what was happening. He took thousands of photographs with the idea of documenting and bearing witness: photos that the artist says he could never again look at. That devastating experience confronted him with the absolute impossibility of representation, which he initially attempted to address through two slightly distanced works: *Signs of Life* and *Untitled (Newsweek)*.[19]

In *Signs of Life*, Jaar adopted a formula that he admired in the work of the Japanese conceptual artist On Kawara – who, during his travels, used to send daily telegrams with the same message: 'I'm still alive!' – and mailed postcards to his friends from tourist sites in Rwanda with the names of the survivors he had come across ('Jyamiya Muhawenimawa is still alive!', 'Caritas Namazuru is still alive!', 'Canisius Nzayisenga is still alive!'), in this way tracing out his own itinerary and his personal involvement in that awful event, in the displacement from *I* to *they*. Here, for Jaar, the name – confronted with the horror of the number – takes on an ethical and political force in terms of the restitution of humanity and dignity. This is the same strategy of rescuing the names used in *La Nube*/*The*

Cloud,[20] dealing with those who lost their lives in the attempt to cross the Tijuana–San Diego border, where the work was performed. In the same vein, and also related to Mexico, it is worth mentioning here the intervention of another Chilean, in this case the writer Roberto Bolaño, whose posthumously published novel *2666*[21] immerses readers in the violence of Ciudad Juárez to confront them with the most atrocious mixture of cruelty and indifference to the grief of so many corpses tortured to death. Indeed, in the chapter 'The Part About the Crimes', Bolaño writes the names of the murdered women with a short history, like a burial rite.[22]

Returning to Jaar, his second work on Rwanda, *Untitled* (*Newsweek*), is a critical study of the refusal of the hegemonic international media to report on the events – and, in conjunction, on the real misinformation we are subjected to in the 'globalized' world. The piece presents in series all the covers of *Newsweek* published during the time of the massacre *before* the magazine finally dedicated a *single* cover to it.[23]

On the problematic of representation that prompted him, over a period of years, to experiment with strategies, Jaar says:

> Rwanda required me to shift my perspective quite radically. I spent six years working on this project, it was trying different strategies of representation. Each project was a new exercise, a new strategy, and a new failure. ... Basically this serial structure of exercises was forced by the Rwandan tragedy and my incapacity to represent it in any way that made sense.[24]

One of those strategies was *Real Pictures*,[25] which consisted of a selection of photographs he had taken, each one 'buried' in a black box. The boxes were then piled up to form monuments of different sizes, like tumuli and archives. On each of the boxes the artist wrote a description of the hidden image:

> Gutete Emerita, 30 years old, is standing in front of the church. Dressed in modest, worn clothing, her hair is hidden in a faded pink cotton kerchief. She was attending mass in the church when the massacre began. Killed with machetes, in front of her eyes, were her husband Tito Kahinamura (40), and her two

sons Muhoza (10) and Matirigari (7). Somehow she managed
to escape with her daughter Marie-Louise Unumararunga (12),
and hid in a swamp for three weeks, only coming out at night
for food. When she speaks about her lost family, she gestures to
corpses on the ground, rotting in the African sun.[26]

The following year, Jaar created one of the most emblematic
works in the series, *The Eyes of Gutete Emerita*,[27] which
reproduces a single image of those eyes that have seen so
much on a million slides. The final work consisted of an
installation presided over by Gutete's eyes, where the slides
were piled on a light table with recorded ambient sound
reflecting the context and the history. He employed the same
procedure in *The Silence of Nduwayezu*,[28] with a five-year-
old child in the Rubavu refugee camp a month after the
end of the massacre; the child had also seen a great deal,
including the killing of his family, and had been unable to
speak for some time. Jaar took the image of his eyes – the
saddest he had ever seen, he confessed – and reproduced it in
a very grainy format that gave a hazy effect, and once again
in unbearable numbers, reflecting the context in which the
work had emerged.

> I want to show this child's eyes. But that image will very quickly
> disappear from the public mind. What can I do to keep it there ...
> It has to be spectacular but make sense too. I'm suggesting: this
> is what you need to know. And then I offer you this image in the
> hope that, backed up by the text, it will be very powerful. And
> works fail. Because they're either too weighted toward infor-
> mation or toward spectacle. How do you strike such a perfect
> balance that it's informative, moving, inspires people to think
> and act ... I've no idea how you do it.[29]

In 1988, Alfredo Jaar left Chile for New York, where he
now lives and continues his artistic career. He recently had a
retrospective in Chile in which he showed, among others, the
above work. In 2010, he also accepted an invitation from the
Museo de la Memoria y los Derechos Humanos in Santiago
to produce a permanent exhibit, which he called *Geometría
de la Conciencia* (*The Geometry of the Conscience*) and
which could be described as the infinity of the number
without name.

To view the piece, visitors must descend one floor from the lobby of the museum and enter a subterranean space whose door closes hermetically, leaving them in darkness. Then, in the half-light, they are confronted with featureless faces projected onto a black background, reflected to infinity by mirrors on the lateral walls. After a time, these shapes are illuminated by an intense light for a few seconds, producing a sense of immensity. The forms, the shapes, the outlines, are both the faces of the disappeared and those of present-day pedestrians whose photographs were taken in the street. The concept is that memory lives in the present and within each and every one of us. Or rather, it could be said, that the 'victim' is the whole society which, through the disappearance of so many stories, has suffered the loss of a shared world: that the victim, beyond her face and name, is a universal category. And that memory – our memory – should also find a space, whatever our immediate environment, for our particular traumatic experiences. But the impact of the piece to some extent involves perplexity: our sensibilities and thoughts, here in the twenty-first century, take us beyond frontiers to regard that 'pain of others', as Susan Sontag[30] would have us do, as a species of global citizenship. But at the same time there is a sense that the individual faces with their features, smiles and habitual expressions should not be erased, as those hundreds of gazing photographs seem to request. These are the dilemmas of memory and biographies that we should not, perhaps, attempt to resolve.

Silence, names

The particularity of the work of memory of the recent past in Argentina privileged the genre of testimony, to which a wide variety of other narratives (verbal, audiovisual, autobiographical, [auto]fictional) were later added, forming, in conjunction with reportage, debate and academic research, a very extensive field. Multiple records with time show generational marks, the print of dissimilarity at a distance from the events, their echoes in the voices of those who came later.

Despite so many words, there is also silence. The silence of places of memory in their strict emptiness. The silence of the former clandestine detention centres, including the former ESMA, with its squalid tour of staircases, landings, rooms, shadowy corners, where the act of visiting is itself almost sacrilege. But also the silence of the memorials, constructed for the purpose of 'making remembered'.

Among such memorials is what could unofficially be called 'the wall of names' (officially, the Monumento a las Víctimas del Terrorismo de Estado [Monument to the Victims of State Terrorism]) in Parque de Memoria, a large estate beside the Río de la Plata in Buenos Aires. The symbolism is clear: truncated, discontinuous walls, looking out onto the river – a river over which flew the 'death planes' that ejected live, drugged bodies; walls with thousands of names chiselled into the stone, the names of the disappeared and the dead, simply accompanied by the date of their kidnapping or disappearance, plus their age – a heart-rending statistic of early youth – and the no less chilling addition of 'pregnant' in numerous cases.

There are no photographs, although for the past forty years these have populated many other locations: squares, streets, walls, placards, demonstrations, the famous headscarves of the Madres de Plaza de Mayo and the unmistakable blue strip with thousands of portraits that hundreds of hands carry on every anniversary. The silence allows for individual introspection, remembrance, paying tribute. The names resist epitaphs. Some visitors place flowers on them or take photographs with the background image of the wall. Despite the asymmetry, the wall finally leads to the unbroken horizon of the river. An esplanade briefly juts out into the water, just far enough to give an impression of distance.

Planned in tune with the concept of anti-monumentalism – the function of which has less to do with any hypothetical restoration and closure than to signal emptiness and lack – to stimulate the disquiet of memory rather than to calm it, the wall of names – at the limit of the city – can be thought of as the other face of the voice and also as a virtual narrative that only unfolds in the presence of the other, establishing a particular form of interlocution. A mute interlocution that is primarily hearing – the tympan, again – the attraction of those names that enclose so many lived and truncated lives, so much *being at the limit*, whose singularity, still unconsoled, resists disappearance.

Notes

All translations of citations are by Christina MacSweeney unless otherwise marked.

Introduction

1 Arfuch (2005).
2 Following the 1985 trial of the military juntas in Argentina, which produced a number of convictions of human rights violators, the 1986 'Full Stop Law' (*Ley de Punto Final*, law number 23492) effectively put an end to prosecutions. The 1987 'Due Obedience Law' (*Ley de Obediencia Debida*, law number 23521) held that lower-ranking members of the military and police forces could not be prosecuted because they were thought to have been following the orders of their superiors. Both of these laws were repealed by the National Congress of Argentina in August 2003 but dominated the political and judicial landscape for nearly two decades.
3 This quote comes from an unpublished lecture that Leonor Arfuch delivered at the 14th World Congress on Semiotics (14 Congreso Mundial de Semiótica), 'Trayectorias', held in Buenos Aires in September 2019. For this occasion, she prepared a talk titled 'La semiótica como transdisciplina: análisis, crítica y política' ['Semiotics as Transdiscipline: Analysis, Critique, Politics'].

4 See Arfuch (1992) and *La entrevista: una invención dialógica* (Buenos Aires: Ediciones Paidós, 2010).
5 See Arfuch (2002).
6 See, especially, Lejeune (1975), Paul de Man, 'Autobiography as De-facement', *MLN* 94(5) (December 1984): 919–30, and Molloy (1991).
7 See chapter 3 in this book in which Arfuch cites Michael Holroyd, *Basil Street Blues* (London: Little, Brown, and Company, 1999), pp. 13–14.
8 Arfuch (2013).
9 See chapter 2, third section, in this book.
10 See 'La semiótica como transdisciplina' ['Semiotics as Transdiscipline']. In the original, Arfuch writes about autobiography as 'la búsqueda de cercanía frente al anonimato y la uniformidad de las vidas corrientes' ['the search for closeness in the face of anonymity and the uniformity of ordinary lives'].
11 See Butler (2004, 2005).
12 For this reference, see the ending to Arfuch's 'Prologue' to this book.
13 Arfuch draws special attention to texts like Gilmore (1994) and Smith (2002).

Prologue

1 Butler (2004).
2 Loraux (2002).
3 Molloy and Siskind (2006).
4 Bachelard (1964).
5 Holroyd (2002).
6 Sebald (2001).
7 *Storage Area of the Children's Museum*, Musée d'Art Moderne de la Ville de Paris (1989).
8 [Tr.: The text here refers to the children of those disappeared under the dictatorship, often adopted by military families. The Abuelas de Plaza de Mayo has managed to locate 130 of the 400 children in this situation, and so enable them to recover their true identities.]
9 Actis et al. (2006).
10 Calveiro (2006).
11 Belzagui (2010 [2007]). Extracts from this debate can be found in the *Journal of Latin American Cultural Studies* 16(2) (2007).
12 See Todorov (1984).

13 [Tr.: ESMA: Escuela de Mecánica de la Armada, generally translated as the Navy Petty-Officers School of Mechanics, was a
clandestine detention centre, infamous for torture and extermination in Buenos Aires.]

Chapter 1 A Beginning

1 Derrida (1982).
2 Arfuch (2002).
3 Sarlo (2005).
4 Giddens (1993).
5 Berlant (1998).
6 Mouffe (2005).
7 A weight that, according to Hannah Arendt (1958), is expressed
through *conduct*, as a parameter that underlies the order of
modern society and permeates both the public and the more
recondite intimate spheres.
8 Arfuch (2010a).
9 While in the seventies, Roland Barthes announced 'the death
of the author' and her/his replacement by the textual figure of
the storyteller, which structuralism planted firmly in the realm
of literary criticism, thus weakening the influence of biography,
today those flesh-and-blood authors are expected to talk about
their lives and works in interviews and at book launches, giving
preference to autobiographical elements.
10 There has been a notorious rise in 'genetic criticism', which
studies these manuscripts and drafts as a means of accessing the
creative process through textual transfiguration (marks that will
surely be lost in a future of computers and the possible disappearance of early versions of the final text).
11 Two recent examples are: the publication of Roland Barthes'
Mourning Diary (2010b), composed of the notes he took on the
death of his mother in 1977 (he himself died in 1980); and Julio
Cortázar's *Papeles inesperados* [*Unexpected Writings*] (2009),
which consists of notes and papers found in his library.
12 Cases where biography and (trauma-related) memory are strongly
articulated include: Hannah Arendt and Martin Heidegger
(2004), *Letters 1925–1975*; the letters from Heidegger to his
wife Elfride (1915–1970), published as *Letters to His Wife*
(2008), and the correspondence between Ingeborg Bachmann
and Paul Celan in *Correspondence* (2010).
13 Georges Perec is an emblematic author of this type of narrative.
In a note to a new Argentinian edition of his famous (and

peculiar) autobiography *Je suis né* [*I am Born*] (1990), the critic Jorge Fondebrider (2012) comments:

> Since Georges Perec's untimely death in 1982, so far no less than eighteen new volumes have been published under his name, to be added to the seventeen titles published during his lifetime. These posthumous books, ordered thematically, include everything from individual articles to true stories, interviews, letters, the text of postcards, personal notes, prologues, review articles, transcriptions of lectures, replies to questionnaires and a wide variety of footnotes. And that is not the end of the matter: we are still far from having finished with the great quantity of texts that Perec scattered around the world in the 46 years of his life.

14 Wittgenstein (1953).
15 Bakhtin (1990), p. 152.
16 Bakhtin (1990), p. 152. [Italics in the original.]
17 See, for example, Todorov (2008), Vattimo (2010) and Augé (2011).
18 In relation to this 'beyond', which is not only temporal but also traumatic due to the mark it leaves on various generations, see Davoine and Gaudillière (2004).
19 Todorov (2000).
20 Yerushalmi et al. (1989).
21 Examples of this growing trend can be seen in the work of the Chilean artist Alfredo Jaar, who practises a form of conceptual art in conflict zones (Rwanda, Palestine), in which photography plays a major role; or the French press photographer Luc Dalahaye who, from Iraq, Bosnia and Russia, has developed his *métier* into something recognized as art. See also Didi-Huberman et al. (2007).
22 Rancière (1999).
23 Subjects on the margins to the extent that they are not even excluded within a society in which they are, simultaneously, included in other accounts: public politics, unemployment benefits, philanthropic organizations, etc.

Chapter 2 The Gaze as Autobiography: Time, Place, Objects

1 Holroyd (2002), p. 31.
2 Heidegger (2001).
3 Bachelard (1964).
4 Massey (2005), p. 9.

5 Chantal Akerman's classic and unsettling film *Jeanne Dielman, 23 quai du Commerce, 1080 Bruxelles [Jeanne Dielman, 23 Commerce Quay, 1080 Brussels]* (1975) focuses on these domestic chores, the protagonist's endless labour in the hallways, in the laundry room, in the kitchen, places where no other camera would linger, and that define, in the gaze of that camera, *filming as a woman.*

6 De Certeau (1984), p. 93.

7 The documentary film-maker Jonas Mekas reflected on this in his *A Letter from Greenpoint* (2009), while he was saying his farewell to the loft he had lived in for decades, walking through the space with a digital camera and evoking the presence of 'atoms, totally invisible' of the people who had passed through there and formed a part of the spirit of the place.

8 Sennet (1990) dedicates a chapter of *The Conscience of the Eye* to a historical analysis of the difference between the interior, the 'refuge' of the home, and the exterior, which, in the Judeo-Christian tradition, involves the 'terrors of exposure', homelessness and need (see 'The Refuge', pp. 5–40).

9 De Certeau (1984), p. 103.

10 Barthes (1983).

11 De Certeau (1984), p. 108.

12 Robin (2009).

13 Heidegger (1971), p. 227.

14 Barthes (1979b), p. 58.

15 Ricoeur (1992).

16 Sebald (1998).

17 Within the Bakhtinian concept of polyphony, Authier sees a distinction between constitutive heterogeneity, referring to the diverse voices that speak within a single voice, without being identified, and shown heterogeneity, where the inscription of the word/*parole* of others is explicit: references, allusions, the use of inverted commas, the inclusion of expressions in foreign languages etc.

18 Authier (1982).

19 In Grant Gee's documentary film *Patience (After Sebald)* (2012), the director juxtaposes black and white with colour, images from Sebald's walking tour with voice-over by people who knew or wrote about the author, in some way capturing the double plot on which the book is based.

20 Sebald (1998), p. 35.

21 De Man (1984), pp. 67–81.

22 Sebald was a professor at the University of East Anglia and founded the British Centre for Literary Translation there. He

lived in Norwich until his death in a car crash in December 2001.

23 Sebald (1998), pp. 78–9.

24 Sebald (1998), pp. 38–9.

25 W. G. Sebald (2004). The title has an echo of Benjamin's distinction between 'human history' and 'natural history' in his well-known essay *The Storyteller*, showing the clear influence that author had on Sebald's work. In his introduction to the Spanish edition of the essay, Pablo Oyarzún says: 'What the storyteller does is to re-inscribe human history in natural history, appealing precisely to death as an authority, the place, the event in which one and the other cross in an absolute unresolved manner.'

26 W. G. Sebald (2004), pp. 71–3.

27 Ibid.

28 [Tr.: This reference does not appear in the English edition.]

29 Sebald (1998), p. 283.

30 Ibid., p. 283.

31 Lejeune (1975). The concept of the autobiographical pact refers to the pragmatic functioning of genre, that is, the particular author–narrator identity relationship that autobiography proposes for the reader, under the guarantee of the proper name, which also involves the referential adaptation of the spoken word in the 'retrospective record in prose' of the experience. The author himself has modified the concept in later works to include the multiple forms that inhabit biographical space, but which do not meet those requirements.

32 'Las cosas': ¡Cuántas cosas, / limas, umbrales, atlas, copas, clavos, / nos sirven como tácitos esclavos, / ciegas y extrañamente sigilosas! / Durarán más allá de nuestro olvido; / no sabrán nunca que nos hemos ido. *Elogio de la sombra* (1969), Argentina: EMEMÉ.

33 *JLG/JLG: Self-Portrait in December* (1995).

34 Gadamer (1975).

35 Barthes (1977).

36 In his now classic book, Barthes moves away from the traditional model of autobiographical narrative by the use of the third person, the absence of chronological detail and events, and an emphasis on the work of reading – and, hence, of writing – in the configuration of a biography: being in and through the texts.

37 De Man (1984).

38 Without any attempt to be representative – any selection is necessarily arbitrary and random – there is someone closer to the Latin American experience who succeeded admirably in

bringing objects, time, memory and place together in one work: Nury González, the Chilean visual artist who, in the Chile Triennial (2009) interpreted the theme of the event, *The Chile Earthquake*, by an installation called *Sueño velado* [*Waking Dream*], for which she borrowed bedside tables from friends and acquaintances, with all the objects usually to be found on these items of furniture. In a large salon of Santiago's Museo de Arte Contemporáneo Quinta Normal, she arranged 45 lit lamps, each on its corresponding bedside table, and other objects, in a work of great visual and emotional impact. The diversity of lights, styles, colours and objects, aesthetically arranged in almost magical coexistence, offered a narrative journey with an itinerary that each person could choose at will and read (semiotically) modes of habitation, eras, social classes, tastes, preferences, belongings, imagining the hypothetical users of those small spaces of intimacy that nevertheless do not seem violated by their appearance in public space, possibly because they succeed in wisely questioning the elusive register of the collective. Indeed, the notion of relating the bedside table and the earthquake, possibly the most emblematic figure of Chilean territorial – and national? – identity, intensely evoked for me the lived experience of the feared moment of being shaken from sleep, turning on the light, looking at the clock, jumping out of bed and judging the seriousness of the event, deciding what to do next, what to do in the face of the – repeated – threat of death: the installation is aptly named *Sueño velado* [Tr.: The title plays on the similarity in Spanish between *velado*, the past participle of the verb *velar*, to keep a vigil, and *velador*, which can refer to a 'bedside table'.]. All this and much more was expressed by the illuminated tables in the calm of the exhibition, with its objects marked by time and use (books, clocks, medicines, papers, memories). An anonymous biographical space – minimal, singular, objectual biographies – that condensed a strong cultural identity and a shared memory. See online: http://www.nurygonzalez.uchile.cl.

39 Boltanski and Grenier (2009), pp. 80–1.

40 Ibid., pp. 144–5.

41 In 2010, Boltanski held two exhibitions on the same theme but varying with the venue: Grand Palais de Paris, Monumenta, *Personnes*, which can translate as both 'person' and 'nobody'; the New York exhibition was called, *No Man's Land*. In both cases, 30 tons of clothing, arranged in rectangles on the floor, separated by walkways, and one large 30-metre-high pile, where a mechanical arm – the hand of God? – picked up items of

clothing and let them fall to the ambient sound of a heartbeat. The obvious references were disappearance, death and the Shoah, but also contemporary anonymity and uniformity, that chance involved in any trajectory. Its monumental character, the spectacle, make it particularly vulnerable to criticism, and the artist himself suggested that it could have a very strong effect on the public.

42 Ibid., p. 78
43 Ibid., p. 124.
44 Ibid., p. 163–4.
45 Unexpectedly in tune with this, and vouching for the above, shortly after this book was finished a multi-space exhibition of Boltanski's work was opened, organized by the Universidad de Tres de Febrero (UNTREF), curated by Diana Wechsler. Two of the pieces were original works, made in emblematic memory sites in the city: *Migrantes* [*Migrants*], an installation/intervention in the old Hotel de Immigrantes [Immigrants' Hotel], in the port area, where those who travelled from far corners of the world to populate these lands used to stay for a short time on their arrival; and *Flying Books*, an installation in the former Biblioteca Nacional. In *Migrantes*, Boltanski used the stripped-down, abandoned building with its slightly sinister air to install the sensitive objects traditionally associated with his work (chairs with coats draped over their backs or hanging as silhouettes, old beds, illuminated from within, lined up in a room), all this in semi-darkness, only interrupted by evocative lamps and whispering voices speaking a variety of languages, with the names and places of origin of real immigrants taken from the archives. The scene ended in a long corridor with soft lighting, evoking exhausting journeys with no certain end, presences/absences that also relate to contemporary journeys. *In Flying Books*, which was shown in the large reading room of the historic library, hundreds of books floated in an empty space of great architectural value, evoking not only past time and absence in a place famous for its accumulation of knowledge (this library, of which Borges was the most illustrious director, inspired the author's short story 'The Library of Babel') but perhaps also, and not without a touch of nostalgia, the long-foretold demise of the paper book.

The Tecnópolis science and art park housed a section of his global recording *Les archives du Coeur* [*Archives of the Heart*], heartbeats collected in various points around the world and preserved on a Japanese island for a hypothetical posterity, and a selection of the above-mentioned works was shown in the

Museo de la UNTREF. This selection included: *Mon Coeur* [*My Heart*], a dark room only illuminated by a single light flickering to the rhythm of the artist's heart; *Monument*, his classic altars of photographs and light bulbs; *Réserve* [*Reserve*], a salon whose walls are lined with hung clothes, and 6 *Septembres* (the artist's birthday), which consists of a video installation, images of news broadcasts emitted on that date over the 60 years since his birth. Thousands of images with sound screened at high speed – which the viewer can stop for an instant by pressing a button – once again formed a bridge between the singular autobiography and the one shared with others, in this case the events that make up the memory of the world, a twofold memorial register that constructs us in the historical dimension. The multi-space exhibition *Boltanski in Buenos Aires* was open to the public 12 October–16 December 2012.

46 Ibid., p. 22.
47 Christian Boltanski artwork (1972), *10 Portraits Photographiques de Christian Boltanski, 1946–1964* [*10 Portrait Photographs of Christian Boltanski 1946–1964*].
48 Christian Boltanski artwork (1974), *Les Saynètes Comiques* [*One-act Comedies*].
49 Robin (1996).
50 Boltanski and Grenier (2009), p. 72.
51 Boltanski artwork (1975).
52 Boltanski and Grenier (2009), p. 64.
53 In an article originally published in *Punto de Vista*, I analysed this work, which formed part of an exhibition in the Museo de Bellas Artes de Buenos Aires in March 1996, in relation to our 'collective family album', a title which can be applied to the photos of the disappeared, whose conjunction in marches commemorating the twentieth anniversary of the right-wing military coup of 24 March 1976 is particularly significant. See 'Álbum de familia' ['Family Album'] in Arfuch (2008).
54 Boltanski and Grenier (2009), p. 151.
55 Ibid., p. 197.
56 Ibid., p. 207.
57 [Tr.: The Spanish edition of Holroyd's work on which Arfuch bases this section is a compilation of texts from both these books.]
58 Holroyd remembers Philip Larkin's argument that literary manuscripts have two types of value: magical and meaningful. 'The first, which is older and universal, kindles research with a peculiar excitement and intimacy; the second, which is more technical and modern, contributes to our understanding of

a writer's intentions' (Holroyd 1996, p. xxix). Recovering manuscripts has also become a contemporary passion, as is shown by recent editions of the papers of Roland Barthes, Julio Cortázar and Juan José Saer, among others.

59 In a brief summary of the English tradition, with his characteristic humour ('Great Britain oozes biography to the incomprehension and amusement of the world. It is a speciality of our art as well as literature.'), Holroyd recalls that Richard Holmes, one of the great English biographers, considered places to be as important as letters and documents in the task of giving form – spirit – to a biography.

60 Bakhtin (1990).

61 In the 1970 article 'Out of Print' in *The American Scholar*, the author offers a critical panorama of the British publishing world which, by focusing on the most famous figures, eclipses the work of such excellent writers as Patrick Hamilton, Henry Green, Hugh Kingsmill and Charlotte Mew.

62 In his *Brief Lives*, John Aubrey (1626–1697) addressed the challenge of synthesis in the manner of a portrait artist, capturing a feature, an impression – often visual – to give accounts of the prominent people of his time and from history in a curious collection that includes Francis Bacon, Geoffrey Chaucer, Thomas Cromwell, Descartes, Erasmus, Hobbes, John Milton, Thomas More and William Shakespeare, to name but a few.

63 Aubrey (1987).

64 Holroyd (2002), p. 21.

65 Among the works that give clear examples of those diverse perspectives, one of the most notable is Dosse (2007), who is both a theoretician and historian of biography, and a biographer in his own right, as is shown in his monumental 'intersecting lives' of Deleuze and Guattari (2009).

66 Holroyd (1999), p. 13.

67 Virginia Woolf in ibid., p. 12.

68 Ibid., pp. 13–14.

69 Holroyd (2002), pp. 193–208.

70 Ibid., p. 26.

71 Ibid., p. 234.

72 Holroyd (1999), p. 7.

73 Ricoeur (1984/1985/1988).

74 Holroyd (2002), p. 7.

75 Ibid., p. 26.

76 Benjamin (1968).

77 Holroyd (2002), pp. 30–1.

78 Benjamin (1968), pp. 108–9.
79 Benjamin (1998), p. 18.
80 Arfuch (2002).
81 This refers to Bakhtin's (1978) concept, which points to the essential correlation in literature between time and space (*cronos*: time, *topos*: place) and emotional investment, configured in the organizing axis of the story.
82 Benjamin (1968), p. 84.
83 Simmel (2002).
84 In these symbolic meshes, where the works refract and come into dialogue beyond mutual (re)cognition, in her installation *Sobre la historia natural de la destrucción* [*On the Natural History of Destruction*] (2011), the Chilean artist Nury González weaves the threads linking Sebald and Boltanski anew – non-metaphorically. What follows is a transcription of the text accompanying the exhibit.

ONE. Three Mapuche ponchos bought in Temuco. Hundred-year-old weaves, full of holes that for me signify a sort of textile 'memory'. Like archaeologists who mark out their digs with canvas and stakes, I used white thread to mark each of the 'wounds' on the cloth, transforming the ponchos into a map or route of destruction. Each of them into a text: *Al hilo de la historia* [*The Thread of History*], *Con el alma en un hilo* [*With the Soul on a Thread*] and *Al hilo del pensamiento* [*A Strand of Thought*].

TWO. A video. On the shore of a lake, three curtains from the destroyed Carlton Ritz hotel in Beiruit, draped into the water. A Lebanese artist brought them to Chile for me. The sound is broadcast on the second floor of the salon, where the digital diptychs are shown.

THREE. Three digital diptychs. The images change every 15 seconds. On the left, 15 images of a destroyed city with 15 darned details on a cloth. Centre, 15 images of people fleeing with suitcases across the border with 15 details of those suitcases. On the right, 15 close-up photographs of people wrapped in blankets with 15 blue darned pieces of cloth. Indigo, like Mapuche ponchos ...

Exiles and landless peoples are crossed in the presence of those Mapuche ponchos: the lost land, the lost territories, the lost histories. That is also where the title of this work comes from, *On the Natural History of Destruction*. Apparently everything extraordinary that happens becomes natural. Then, the destruction of all dignity will be normal. My head is filled with that image. (See www.nurygonzalez.uchile.co)

85 Sebald (2004), p. 131.

86 Barthes (1979a), p. 58.

87 [Tr.: Barthes' use of *discrétion* is variously translated as *delicacy* or *tact* in English, whereas in Spanish it is *delicadeza*.]

88 As might be expected, given the prominent position this figure occupies in the Barthesian universe, a number of notes appear in compilations of his papers. In the first volume of *How to Live Together* (2013, p. 124), he quotes de Sade: 'I have tastes for fantasies: however baroque they may be. I find them all respectable, for one is not the master of them, and because the most singular and bizarre of them, when well examined, always depends on a principle of tact.' In another, in *The Neutral* (2005, p. 30), Barthes speaks of tact as: 'Not "traits", "elements", "constituents", but what shines by bursts, in disorder, fugitively, successively, in the "anecdotal" discourse: the weave of anecdotes in the book of life.'

89 Boltanski and Grenier (2009), p. 219.

90 The exhibition, *Mémoire des camps. Photographies des camps de concentration nazis* [*Memoir of Camps. Photographs of Nazi Concentration Camps*], held in Paris in 2001, organized by Clément Chéroux, gave rise to a publication of the same name. Didi-Huberman showed four photographs from the Archives of the Auschwitz-Birkenau State Museum, taken in the camp at great risk by a *Sonderkommando* – as the Jews in charge of the gas chambers were known – with a (fictional) narrative about the vicissitudes of that day when the only photographs in existence of an official close to the gas chambers was taken, in the before and after of his horrendous task. The story and the following barbed polemic were collected in his book *Images in Spite of All* (2008). I addressed the topic in the essay 'Imaginar pese a todo' ['Imagine in Spite of All'] (Arfuch 2008).

91 Didi-Huberman (2008).

92 Boltanski and Grenier (2009), p. 222.

Chapter 3 Memory and Image

1 Nancy (2005), p. 25.

2 Sebald (2001).

3 Sebald (2001), pp. 192–3.

4 Some years after I read Austerlitz, on 5 September 2009 to

be exact, an article appeared in the Buenos Aires daily *Clarín* under the title 'He saved children from Nazism and yesterday he embraced them again'. The article commented on the incredible initiative undertaken by Nicholas Winton, a British man who visited Prague for work in 1938 and had an inkling of the tragedy awaiting Europe after Hitler's advance. He began to organize train journeys from Prague to London's Liverpool Street for young children of Jewish families. 'Winton,' said the article, 'succeeded in scheduling the departure of eight trains, in which 669 children were transported to London for adoption by British families.' The article celebrates the meeting of Winton, a centenarian, and twenty-two of the surviving children, by then elderly, who, with members of their families, had spent three days crossing Europe on a period train to embrace their saviour in London. A photograph of the meeting is included. Evidently Sebald – a conscientious, studious researcher who lived in England for 30 years until his early death in 2001 – knew the story well and constructed his extraordinary character's adventures on the basis of it. [Tr.: In 2006, a statue commemorating the *Kindertransport* was unveiled in Hope Square at the entrance to Liverpool Street Station.]

5 Ibid., p. 194.
6 Ibid., pp. 200–1.
7 Ibid., pp. 258–9.
8 Ricoeur (2004).
9 Nicole Loraux (2002) makes a masterly analysis of the tension between forgetting past misfortunes and the unforgettable in ancient Athens, particularly in the chapter 'Of Amnesty and Its Opposite', a tension that is also present in the contemporary politics of memory.
10 Ricoeur (2004) offers a very thorough investigation of philosophical thought on memory from the ancient Greeks (basically Plato and Aristotle) to Husserl's phenomenology and other contemporary currents.
11 Nancy (2005).
12 This refers to the Bakhtinian conception that unites the double valence of response and responsibility on the ethical plane (Bakhtin 1990), which is similar to that proposed by the Romanian philosopher Emmanuel Levinas (1987).
13 Halbwachs (1992).
14 The notion of anti- or counter-monumentalism was developed in Germany to describe a new tendency in the politics – and aesthetics – of memory, expressed in works that, rather than reconstructing what is lost, make that loss, what cannot be

recovered, visible. Horst Hoheisel, for example, designed the 'hot stone' monument in Buchenwald concentration camp, a concrete slab inscribed with the names of the national groups victimized there, marking the site of the prisoners' wooden memorial obelisk, which later disappeared. The slab is maintained at body temperature (37°C) by a radiant heating system. The same artist redesigned the famous Aschrott fountain, donated by a wealthy Jewish businessman to the city of Cologne in 1908 and later destroyed by the Nazis, leaving its original shape but with the fountain sunken so that the water can only be seen through a grille in the ground. See Young (2000).
15 Bourdieu (1998).
16 Benjamin (1968), pp. 83–110.
17 Nancy (2005), pp. 21–2.
18 I discuss the relationship between art and traumatic memory in Arfuch (2008).
19 Boltanski artwork (1989).

Chapter 4 Women Who Narrate: Autobiography and Traumatic Memories

1 Preliminary versions of this chapter were published in: the journal *Acta Sociológica* 53, (September–December 2010), Universidad Autónoma de México (UNAM), Centro de Estudios Sociológicos; the journal *Tumultes* 36 (May 2011), Université Paris-Diderot; and in V. Tozzi and N. Lavagnino (eds) (2012), *Hayden White. La escritura del pasado y el futuro de la historiografía* [*Hayden White: The Writing of the Past and the Future of Histiography*], Buenos Aires: EDUNTREF.
2 'El narrador': En cuanto cunde el miedo, la penuria o la peste, / la narración se altera en esos puntos donde se quiebra el orden, / y entonces aparecen crónicas de invasiones y derrotas, / episodios oscuros donde hay fieras ocultas y algún otro es el rey / y uno es un fugitivo debajo de la piel, / tal como si habitara en el párrafo intruso de una leyenda negra.
3 Bakhtin (1992), p. 95.
4 White (1987, 2005).
5 Ricoeur (1985).
6 In the 'reconnection', the circuit of communication, I am thinking of the silence imposed by the concentration camp experience (and its aftermath, as a real threat or self-imposed inhibition) but far from any notion of the simple transmission or transference of a meaning. On the contrary, I mean

communication in its radical impossibility, in the constituent dissymmetry of that circuit and, nevertheless, in the constantly renewed attempt to reach the other, in this case the act of *listening* in an almost physical, bodily sense. See Derrida (1982).

7 The primacy of testimony in all its varieties is in marked difference to the Chilean experience, where the Rettig and Valech reports were limited to the recording of facts, without making use of the voice in the story of the experiences of victims and those who mourn their loss. Nelly Richard (2010) highlights the significance of this absence in the collective construction of public memory that reaches beyond institution-alization in museums, monuments or commemorations.

8 CONADEP collected testimony of torture, rape, imprisonment in clandestine detention centres, the seizure of children born in captivity whose parents were then killed, the looting of private residences, the forging of property deeds, a whole criminal panoply of state terrorism seen as crimes against humanity. Those testimonies were published in the book *Nunca más* [*Never Again*] and many of them were later repeated by the witnesses themselves during the historic trial of the former military juntas where, in 1985 and for the first time in Latin America, the main culprits were tried and sentenced to life imprisonment. After this trial, which some called the 'Argentinian Nüremberg', the laws of Punto Final [Full Stop] and Obediencia Debida [Due Obedience] were passed, preventing other repressors from being tried, and then, from 1989 to 1990, pardons were decreed for almost 200 of those found guilty. In 2003, under a different government, claims of unconstitutionality were made against those pardons – backed by the International Court of Justice in The Hague's 1998 declaration, which universally defined 'crimes against humanity' and their imprescriptible character – and finally, in 2005, under the government of Nestor Kirchner, all the so-called 'Laws of Impunity' were repealed, allowing for the (re)opening of the trials, which are still in progress and in which those responsible for the clandestine detention centres are being sentenced, even down to the second ranking repressors and the *grupos de tareas* [task forces] who operated in the centres.

9 The armed wings of the political left – basically, the Ejército Revolucionario del Pueblo [Peoples' Revolutionary Army] and the Montoneros – were already operating in clandestinity, and guerrilla activities had become sporadic by the time the military coup occurred, with fierce repression that fell not only on those armed wings but also on the grassroots militants (*perejiles*),

journalists, intellectuals and, to a lesser extent, even people close to but not directly involved in the militancy.

10 Derrida (2000), p. 195.

11 I am referring again to Benjamin's famous essay 'The Storyteller' (see Benjamin 1968), in which the author notes the horrendous inability to speak experienced by soldiers returning from the front after the First World War with their senses and perceptions severely disturbed and sets out the theory that the loss of experience is linked to the decline of oral narrative and, thus, the circuit of listening, brought about by the growth of the novel and information genres.

12 Among the most important of these films are: *Papá Iván*, directed by María Inés Roqué (2004), *Los rubios*, directed by Albertina Carri (2003) and *M*, directed by Nicolás Prividera (2007).

13 The seizure of the children of the disappeared, born in captivity or kidnapped during raids on houses, assigned to the repressors or their families and to a lesser extent to other 'adopters', is an unprecedented crime against humanity. In this respect, the Abuelas de Plaza de Mayo have undertaken the enormous task of searching for those grandchildren who have been denied the right to their true identity. Of what is calculated to be approximately 500 grandchildren in this situation, up to August 2019, 130 had been identified and recovered by use of the most up-to-date DNA analysis technology. Some young people, alerted by this quest and suspecting themselves not to be the true offspring of their adoptive parents, have themselves approached the Abuelas; others have been found after intensive searches based on specific clues; there are also cases of people who have refused identification, although a law has recently been passed making the genetic confrontation obligatory when there is a presumption of identity.

14 One such equivalence is the 'theory of the two demons', which, by diminishing the principal role of the state in controlling violence by law and justice, explains (and in the worst cases justifies) the latter's crimes by the supposed similarity between the two forms of violence in terms of their lack of concern for the death of the other, the 'enemy', or terms a perfectly organized mechanism for producing the worst torture and humiliation of vulnerable people, including children, as 'excesses'.

More recently, the vindication of 'complete memory' has been claimed by family members and comrades-in-arms, which would include the victims of guerrilla attacks that are also equated with state terrorism. See Salvi (2012), pp. 265–81.

15 Sarlo (2005).
16 De Man (1984).
17 The fluctuation of this figure, depending on how it is seen, clearly evokes Borges' 'The Theme of the Traitor and the Hero', where the two are in fact the same person. On the figure of the traitor in stories of the repression, see Longoni (2007).
18 In Liliana Heker's novel *The End of the Story* (2012), the main character is a militant *montonera* (female urban guerrilla) – presented as an intimate friend of the also female narrator – who is detained in the Escuela de Mecánica de la Armada (ESMA) and tortured. She is believed to have been disappeared but later 'appears' at liberty, in an amorous relationship with her repressor and working to support the political ambitions of an admiral. It is a typical case, not only in Argentina, which brings together in one figure a twofold stigma: passion for the executioner and betrayal. Faced with the emotional impact of this discovery, the friend – identified as the *I* of the narrative voice – who had previously been inconsolable, adopts an attitude of strong moral censure. Heker was harshly criticized because the novel deals with a well-known case, presented in the work with a wealth of 'real' detail, but using aliases. When questioned about the real or fictional nature of the narrative *I* – that is to say, if the novel should be read as autobiographical – Heker's response varied with the occasion, so that the text's 'pact with the reader' and therefore its ethical consequences, were never clearly established.
19 Butler (2004).
20 Ricoeur (2004), p. 176.
21 As new trials related to the former clandestine detention centres are opened, involving repressors not previously tried, and since there is insufficient evidential documentation of their crimes, the testimonies – of both male and female witnesses – are repeated with all their weight of trauma.
22 Several of these works assumed a collective character: in 1996 Marta Diana published a compilation of interviews, *Mujeres guerrilleras. Sus testimonios en la militancia de los setenta* [*Women Guerrilleras: Their Testimonies during the Militancy of the Seventies*]; Noemi Ciollaro published another, *Pájaros sin luz. Testimonios de mujeres de desaparecidos* [*Birds without Light: Testimonies of Wives of the Disappeared*] in 1999; in 2006, Beguán et al.'s *Nosotras, las presas políticas. 1974–1983* [*We, Political Prisoners: 1974–1983*] appeared, a compilation of stories, letters, poems and drawings by the protagonists themselves. In terms of poetry, Susana Romano Sued addressed her concentration camp experience in *Procedimiento. Memoria*

de La Perla y La Rivera [*Procedures: Memory of La Perla and La Rivera*] in 2007.

23 Calveiro (2006).

24 Actis et al. (2006).

25 Curiously, both books have the same year of publication (2006); however, the first was written in 1998, shortly after the twentieth anniversary of the coup; the second was published on the thirtieth anniversary.

26 As mentioned earlier, the ESMA was, paradoxically, the most important naval training school, set in 17 hectares of grounds in an upper-middle-class neighbourhood of Buenos Aires, where hundreds of young people were trained and officers from the interior of the country were accommodated during trips to the capital; these activities continued as normal during the whole period in question. The detention centre was housed in a basement and various floors of the Casino de Oficiales [Officers' Club], where the regular activities of meetings and entertainment coexisted with terrifying torture sessions and the imprisonment of large numbers of detainees, who were hooded and kept in inhumane conditions. Within the centre there was a clandestine maternity ward, where the newly born infants were handed over to whoever was top of a list of applicants; it was also from there that the trucks departed for the 'death flights', on which drugged prisoners were dropped into the sea. The premises also functioned as a 'document centre' where books, newspapers and other material taken during raids were stored alongside a wide range of 'war booty' that hypothetically served to feed – strategically, ideologically – the political ambitions of the then commander-in-chief of the navy, to whose 'support tasks' certain prisoners were assigned before recovering their freedom. In 2005, the whole school was moved and the premises became the Museo de la Memoria [Museum of Memory]. The former detention centre can be visited on a guided tour, and other buildings house the Archivo Nacional de la Memoria [National Memory Archive] and the Centro Cultural Haroldo Conti; two buildings have been assigned to the Madres de Plaza de Mayo, another to the Abuelas, and plans are in progress for other uses of premises.

27 Calveiro (2006), p. 47.

28 Benveniste (1973), p. 221.

29 Calveiro (2006), p. 42. The quotation is from the testimony of Martín Gras to the Comisión Argentina de Derechos Humanos [Argentinian Commission for Human Rights].

30 Ibid., pp. 51–2. The quotation is from the testimonies of Ana

María Sara de Osatinsky and Alicia Milia de Pirles to the French National Assembly.
31 Bakhtin (1990).
32 Calveiro (2006), p. 62.
33 Quoted in Deleuze (2007), p. 187.
34 Barthes (1977). This form of 'anti-autobiography' was supported by only a few verifiable references, some photographs and a selection of texts that disdained the (auto)biographical canon. Barthes proposed that it should be read as the voice of a character in a novel, thus demonstrating the fictional nature of every assumption of the *I*.
35 Actis et al. (2006), p. 22.
36 In the prologue, the authors refer to the silences, interruptions and tears that often assailed them. Their elimination from the final version – one of a number of possible options – is significant in terms of discourse analysis.
37 Gilmore (2001), p. 7.
38 Agamben's (1999) distinction between *terstis* (the witness to something seen or known of) and *superstite* (the person who has experienced the situation, the survivor) is well known.
39 De Man (1984), p. 70.
40 De Man's concept, the idea of a 'mutual reflexive substitution' between both participants in the communication – in reading but also face to face – could be considered to be close to Bakhtin's (1990) 'biographical value', which also involves a value-related tuning in.
41 Some of the detainees were sent to work in government departments, as is the case here.
42 Actis et al. (2006), p. 77.
43 The Capucha was one of the sinister places in the ESMA where the prisoners slept on mattresses on the floor, were hooded and not allowed to speak.
44 The aim of the 'expedition' was the denunciation of a *compañero* seen in the street or some public place; this practice caused the detainees a great deal of anguish.
45 Ibid., p. 78.
46 Ibid., p. 99.
47 Grice (1975).
48 Greimas (1987).
49 Propp (1968).
50 In the second stage of life in the camp, when they had joined the 'Staff', that is, were undertaking the unpaid work of archiving, reading and preparation of material to feed the political ambitions of the head of the Navy, their repressors, in addition to taking

them to dinner – and sometimes dancing – used to accompany the detainees on 'visits' to their families and even sit at table without this having any effect on their fates. The following 'stage' consisted of offering some of them the option of leaving the country, while others were pressured into accepting probation.

51 Gilmore (2001).

52 Among others, Joan Scott (1991, pp. 779–97) addresses this question in her articles 'The Evidence of Experience'. Raymond Williams's (1985) analysis of the use of the term 'experience' in the Anglo-American tradition makes a distinction between knowledge gained from past events and a particular variety of consciousness that can involve both 'reason' and 'knowledge' – which signals the close relationship that still existed in the early eighteenth century between 'experience' and 'experiment'. In the twentieth century, that form of consciousness has come to mean a 'full and active "awareness" including feeling as well as thought ... The notion of experience as subjective witness, writes Williams, is 'offered not only as truth but as the most authentic kind of truth', as 'the ground for all (subsequent) reasoning and analysis'. But it also refers to influences that are external to individuals, which do not include their thought or consideration. According to Scott, this point of departure requires the 'prior existence of individuals' rather than questioning 'how conceptions of self ... are produced' and 'naturalizes categories such as man, woman, black, white, heterosexual and homosexual, by treating them as given characteristics of individuals'. The category of experience needs to be redefined, critically rethought, released from its metaphysical weight as a 'universal' valency, applicable to individuals of any kind. On this point, she addresses Teresa de Lauretis's response, which is summarized in the following footnote.

53 Teresa de Lauretis (1984) undertakes this task in a book covering semiotics, feminism, cinema and representation in an attempt to respond to such questions as how a woman writes or speaks (or makes films). Her notion of experience is, then, linked to the politics of self-representation, the refraction of the constituting and constituted gazes, the ways in which each subject (always provisionally) engages with regulating codes – which, as Judith Butler (1998) stresses, do not operate through external domination but through psychological mechanisms of (self-)subjugation. Semiotics has a leading role in this investigation, in which the construction of a female subject involves not only the (semiotic) interaction of the external and internal spheres in terms of material, economic and interpersonal

relationships, of social and, in the long term, historical events, but also implies a relationship with the body and sexuality. It is in this complex weave of relationships that the social does not blur individual agency – consciousness of self which could be developed in emancipatory political practices – and through those 'technologies of gender' that it becomes possible to speak of the experience (of women).

54 Felski (1989).

55 Gilmore (2001).

56 Gilmore addresses this debate with Felski in *Autobiographics: A Feminist Theory of Women's Self-Representation* (1994, p. 225).

57 The notion of *agency* is used by some feminists to oppose a tendency within feminism to posit women as victims, the mere object of subjection. In this way, stress is laid on women's capacity for action, their strategies for survival, resistance, negotiation, etc. This conception in turn allows feminists to distance themselves from the notion of the autonomy of the free, self-determining subject.

58 The name is not always used in testimonies of women gathered outside trials. That avoidance, which most probably has to do with shame or protection of privacy, is clear in the various voices brought together in the compilations mentioned in footnote 22. The anonymous account, *A Woman in Berlin: Eight Weeks in the Conquered City: A Diary* (2006), is another example of that withholding of the name, while also being a unique documentation of everyday life in that devastated, besieged city, later occupied by the Allies, where German women were subjected to corporal punishment, rape and even murder. In its course, the book (published in Germany in the 1950s and negatively received) once again speaks of the temporalities of memory, of the time that must pass before the recounting of certain traumatic events can be accepted and elaborated by society.

59 According to Paul de Man (1984), the figure of autobiography is, as has been said, prosopopoeia.

60 Gilmore (1994).

61 Didi-Huberman (2008).

62 Benveniste (1973), p. 3.

63 Bakhtin (1993).

64 I address this topic in *La entrevista, una invención dialógica* [*The Interview: A Dialogic Invention*] (2010a).

65 An early example of this combination was undoubtedly Miguel Bonasso's novel *Recuerdo de la muerte* [*Remembrance of Death*] (1984).

66 Under the term 'witness literature', Hayden White (2005) gathers the various generic expressions of traumatic experiences, including the most canonical testimonies. My reference to literature makes a poetic distinction in relation to other expressions.

Chapter 5 Political Violence, Autobiography and Testimony

1 The first versions of this chapter appeared in Ginzburg, Hardman and Seligman-Silva (2012); and Huffschmidt and Durán (2012).
2 Belzagui (2010 [2007]).
3 Belzagui (2010 [2007]).
4 The interview was published in October and November 2004 and del Barco's letter in December of the same year; the replies appeared in *La Intemperie* and other magazines and internet sites throughout 2005, and a large number of articles on the topic were published in 2006.
5 Bakhtin (1990), p. 18.
6 Del Barco (2007).
7 In a second stage, the same and other authors published articles in the above-mentioned magazines, which were then compiled in the first book.
8 Habermas (1989).
9 The second volume, however, contains essays by Claudia Hilb and Victoria Basualdo.
10 Letter written by Héctor Schmucler. See Belzagui (2010 [2007]), pp. 80 and 81.
11 Vezzetti (2009).
12 Belzagui (2010 [2007]), p. 326.
13 Ibid., p. 77.
14 Tatián (2007).
15 Foster in Belzagui (2010 [2007]), p. 282.
16 In this respect, see Friedländer (1992).
17 Laclau (2000).
18 Butler (2004).
19 Benjamin (1968), p. 255.
20 I analysed the performative impact of this media confession in an article in *Punto de Vista* (1995), then republished in Arfuch (2008).
21 An interesting reflection on the possibility of – need for – the word in relation to traumatic experience, based on the actions

of truth commissions throughout the world, can be found in Hayner (2001).
22 Vezzetti (2009).
23 Bakhtin (1993).
24 Belzagui (2010 [2007]), p. 77.
25 Butler (2005).

Chapter 6 The Threshold, the Frontier: Explorations at the Limits

1 The first version of this chapter was a paper presented at the Seminario Giros Teóricos IV 'Lenguaje, transgresión y fronteras' [Language, Transgression and Frontiers], at the Instituto de Investigaciones sobre la Universidad y la Educación of the Universidad Nacional Autónoma de México (UNAM/IISUE), 21–24 February 2012; and in the Iberian and Latin American Cultures Department of Stanford University, 28 February 2012.
2 Anzaldúa (1987).
3 '*Chicano* is a term employed colloquially, principally in the United States, to refer to Mexican-Americans. It was initially used to refer to Hispanic people settled in United States territories that had previously belonged to Mexico (Texas, Arizona, New Mexico, California, Utah, Nevada and parts of Colorado and Wyoming). However, depending on the source and context, it can also refer to a United States citizen of Mexican origins or a person born in the United States of Mexican origin' [Tr.: excerpt from Wikipedia included by the author]. It is interesting to see in this text the subtle variations of naming that must undoubtedly affect social and institutional life. Anzaldúa, for her part, was the daughter of seventh-generation Texan farmworkers and suffered discrimination and racism from childhood.
4 This is an everyday saga captured by infrared cameras in the dehumanization of faceless figures moving in a geological map, as shown by Chantal Akerman in her film *De l'autre côté* (2002). According to the Belgian director, the project had its origins in the news that certain Arizona ranchers had decided to take the law into their own hands rather than denouncing the undocumented immigrants who had managed to cross the frontier to border patrols. She decided to film the final part of a trilogy (a sort of travel diary that had previously included Eastern Europe and the American South) at the limit between Mexico and the United States, collecting the stories of migrants and the families

of victims, traces of everyday life and the landscape from a perspective mixing documentary and anthropology.

5 Massey (2005).

6 'The San Ysidro Port of Entry (San Diego-Tijuana) is one of the largest land border crossings in the world. In 2005, 41,417,164 people entered the United States through the frontier post. The great majority of them are Mexican and American workers who live in Tijuana and work in San Diego and Southern California. The time needed to cross the San Ysidro Port of Entry is notoriously long, particularly for those entering the United States by car.' (Taken from a Spanish-language Wikipedia page [Tr.: I have translated the Spanish page as the information given in English is different.])

   By contrast, the crossing into Mexico is simple, and there is practically no control for pedestrians. It should also be pointed out that it is the most highly militarized frontier crossing between the two nations, with a double wall in some stretches, constant patrols on the United States side and the deployment of control technologies usually only used in war.

7 Lash (2007).

8 Smith (1996).

9 Lipovetsky and Serroy (2008).

10 Ludmer (2011).

11 Bakhtin (1990), pp. 137, 103.

12 The participating artists were: Ignasi Aballí, Dennis Adams, Ursula Biemann, Hannah Collins, Jordi Colomer, Francesco Jodice, Rogelio López Cuenca, Antoni Muntadas and Krzysztof Wodiczko.

13 Guasch (2010), p. 13.

14 'inSite emerged in 1992 as an experience of cultural erosion and mapping of interstices in the Tijuana–San Diego border area. Later installations and site-specific artefacts were produced with the aim of provoking local reflection on the limit as a critical emplacement between Mexican and United States contemporary artists and institutions. Very soon the frontier not only showed itself as a place ravaged by harsh identity processes but, in turn, that peripheral border itself became a hub in the operative framework of globalisation.' [Tr.: the link to this quotation no longer exists. However, further information on inSite can be found at: https://modernlatinamericanart. wordpress.com/2013/05/09/insite-san-diego/.]

   Over the years, artists, many of them internationally renowned, projected their work 'on-site', which was preferably the Mexican side of the frontier. There were also activities in the San Diego region but in enclosed spaces with smaller audiences. Néstor García Canclini (2003) carried out research on these practices in the years 1994, 1997 and 2000–2001. The programme's last initiative was inSite 05, in which Muntadas participated.

15 The Mexican channel Televisa transmitted the work on Canal 12. I have no information on whether or not it was shown in the United States.

16 In an example of this 'turn', under the aegis of the European Network of Public Art Producers (ENPAP), a symposium was held (22–24 March, 2012) in a number of localities in the Basque Autonomous Community (principally Bilbao and Vitoria-Gasteiz) under the title *Going Public – Telling It As It Is?* The central thesis was that 'storytelling has always been an extremely important element and can be employed as a methodology for creating and interpreting public art, in continual dialogue with a changing context and local history. Through a series of performative meetings, the symposium explores stories and storytelling as a methodological tool in relation to art in the public sphere.' See: https://www.consonni.org/es/proyectos/enpap-european-network-public-art-producers-going-public-telling-it-it.

17 Muntadas's project notes. See: https://www.macba.cat/global/exposiciones/docs/muntadas/muntada_angl.pdf.

18 Muntadas artwork (2007).

19 [Tr.: *Pateras*: small boats often used by migrants to make the crossing.]

20 Krzysztof Wodiczko artwork (2002).

21 Krzysztof Wodiczko artwork (1999).

22 Krzysztof Wodiczko. Available at: http://krzysztofwodiczko.blogspot.com/p/artwork.html.

23 The roundness of the building – part of an ambitious architectural project – makes the effect of the projected images, outsize heads, even more impressive.

   The purpose was to use progressive technology to give voice and visibility to the women who work in the 'maquiladora' industry in Tijuana. We designed a headset that integrated a camera and a microphone, allowing the wearer to move while keeping the transmitted image in focus. The headset was connected to two projectors and loudspeakers that transmitted the testimonies live. The women's testimonies focused on a variety of issues including work-related abuse, sexual abuse, family disintegration, alcoholism, and domestic violence. These problems were shared live by the participants, in a public plaza on two consecutive nights, for an audience of more than 1,500 projections on the 60-foot diameter facade of the Omnimax Theater at the Centro Cultural Tijuana (CECUT). (Available at: http://web.mit.edu/idg/cecut.html)

24 Mouffe (2007).

25 In bringing together the issue of artistic practices and the hegemonic conception of the political (Laclau and Mouffe 2001), Mouffe is pointing out that these two spheres – art and politics – cannot be separated since all art has a political dimension and the political has an aesthetic dimension. From this comes her rejection of the domination of 'political art' and her preference for the concept of 'critical art' (Mouffe 2007).

26 For Mouffe, the latter tendency is related to the conception of the masses developed by Negri and Hardt.

27 Arendt (1958).

28 Levinas (1985), p. 86.

29 Alÿs artworks (2005 and 1997). See Alÿs's website: http://www. francisalys.com/.

30 Alÿs artwork (1997).

31 Jaar (2006). The piece is available at: http://www.alfredojaar. net/index1.html.

32 Deutsche (2007) [Tr.: I have been unable to access the English version and so have made a back translation from Marcelo Expósito's Spanish.]

33 For example, one of Alÿs's most recent works, *Reel/Unreel* (20 mins), about the burning of films by the Taliban, was filmed in Kabul, Afghanistan in 2011 with the participation of local children and can be accessed online at: http://www.francisalys. com.

34 Mouffe (2007).

35 Néstor García Canclini (2003).

36 In addition to the temperature, Tijuana's online newspaper reports the estimated waiting time for crossing to San Diego, which is usually two to three hours.

37 In some way, this work also repeats Muntadas's attempt to show the 'two sides': after my lecture, it was screened in the Iberian and Latin American Cultures Department of Stanford University to an audience of Chicano, Latino and United States students; it was shown again later during a series of seminars I gave at the Universidad Iberoamericano, Mexico City. In both cases, it was very well received and generated interesting debate.

38 Muntadas in an interview with Pedro Medina in Agra and Zappa (2007, p. 604).

39 Ibid.

40 Alÿs (2007).
41 Arfuch (2008), pp. 27–41.

Chapter 7 The Name, the Number

1 Cavarero (2009).
2 Ibid.
3 Burucúa (2007).
4 Sebald (2004).
5 Mitchell (1996).
6 Boltanski artwork (1989).
7 Calveiro (2006).
8 Actis et al. (2006).
9 In relation to the conversations, see the fragments quoted on pp. 64–6.
10 Jouvé had strongly opposed the 'execution' of those companions, who, according to their leaders, threatened the safety of the group due to their personal or unconscious weakness.
11 Del Barco (2007).
12 Levinas (1985), pp. 100–1.
13 Wodiczko artwork (1999).
14 Jaar artwork (1994–7).
15 The video can be seen at: http://video.mit.edu/watch/hiroshima-projection-4296/.
16 Deutsche (2007), pp. 10–11. The English language version of the text can be found at: http://www.forumpermanente.org/Members/jmbarreto/the-art-of-witness-in-the-wartime-public-sphere/
17 Butler (2004), p. 32.
18 Jaar artwork (1994–7).
19 Jaar artworks (1994 and 1994).
20 Jaar artwork (2000).
21 Bolaño (2008).
22 In her nuanced analysis of the novel, María Stegmayer (2012, p. 58) states:

> possibly one of the most 'expressive' marks of capitalism is its brutal treatment of corpses in an environment that shows itself more strongly where there are no burial rites. The disappearance of the body – an emblematic mark of the atrocious Latin American dictatorships – also appears as an operation typical of the 'narco-machine', as Rossana Reguillo (2012) terms it, and other contemporary forms of organized crime – illegal trafficking of

humans and goods, slave labour, etc. – and becomes the macabre reverse of those situations in which there is a body, or the remains of one, but no name. Anonymous bodies next to names still demand the possibility of being mourned, even though the mourners sometimes cannot even reclaim the bodies. The strategy of allegorical reading that Benjamin calls natural history runs through my analysis of 'The Part About the Crimes' [a novel included in 2666] by Roberto Bolaño, whose writing does justice to the singularity of those bodies. Destroyed bodies, dehumanized remains, the product of both the deregulation and exploitation of work by women in Ciudad Juárez and, as was said, the 'narco-machine' and its ferocious omnipotence in frontier zones. Those lives that, as Butler (2005) says, are not recognized as such and, hence, 'will not even qualify as "grievable," are mourned, find a species of burial rite in the writing'.

23 Jaar showed this work on his last visit to Buenos Aires on 31 July 2012 at the invitation of the Parque de la Memoria of the Universidad Nacional de Tres de Febrero (UNTREF).
24 Schweizer (2007), p. 13.
25 Jaar artwork (1995).
26 Schweizer (2007), p. 13.
27 Jaar artwork (1996).
28 Jaar artwork (1997).
29 Jaar (2006), p. 83.
30 Sontag (2003).

Bibliography

Actis, Munú, Aldini, Cristina, Gardella, Liliana, Lewin, Miriam and Tokar, Elisa (2006) *That Inferno: Conversations of Five Women Survivors of an Argentine Torture Camp*, trans. Gretta Siebentritt. Nashville: Vanderbilt University Press.

Agamben, Giorgio (1999) *Remnants of Auschwitz: The Witness and the Archive*, trans. Daniel Heller-Roazen. New York: Zone Books.

Agra, Rocío and Zappa, Gustavo (2007) *Con/textos Dos. Muntadas. Una antología crítica* [*Con/texts Two. Muntadas: A Critical Anthology*]. Buenos Aires: Nueva Librería.

Alÿs, Francis (2007) *Sometimes Doing Something Poetic Can Become Political and Sometimes Something Political Can Become Poetic*. New York: David Zwimmer.

Anon. (2006) *A Woman in Berlin: Eight Weeks in the Conquered City: A Diary*, trans. Philip Boehm. New York: Picador.

Anzaldúa, Gloria (1987) *Borderlands/La Frontera: The New Mestiza*, trans. Norma Cantú. San Francisco: Aunt Lute Books.

Arce, Luz (2004) *The Inferno: A Story of Terror and Survival in Chile*, trans. Stacey Alba Skar. Madison: University of Wisconsin Press.

Arendt, Hannah (1958) *The Human Condition*. Chicago: University of Chicago Press.

Arendt, Hannah and Heidegger, Martin (2004) *Letters 1925–1975*, trans. Andrew Shields. Boston: Harcourt.

Arfuch, Leonor (1992) *La interioridad pública* [*Public Intimacy*].

Buenos Aires: Universidad de Buenos Aires, Facultad de Ciencias Sociales.

Arfuch, Leonor (1995) 'Confesiones, conmemoraciones' ['Confessions and Commemorations'], in *Punto de Vista* 52: 6–11; and in Leonor Arfuch (2008), *Crítica cultural entre política y poética* [*Cultural Criticism between Political and Poetic*]. Buenos Aires: Fondo de Cultura Económica, pp. 27–41.

Arfuch, Leonor (2002) *El espacio biográfico. Dilemas de la subjetividad contemporánea.* [*The Biographical Space: Dilemmas of Contemporary Subjectivity*]. Buenos Aires: Fondo de Cultura Económica.

Arfuch, Leonor (2005) *Pensar este tiempo. Espacios, afectos, pertenencias* [*To Think This Time: Space, Affections, Belonging*]. Buenos Aires: Paidós.

Arfuch, Leonor (2008) *Crítica cultural entre política y poética* [*Cultural Criticism between Politics and Poetics*]. Buenos Aires: Fondo de Cultura Económica.

Arfuch, Leonor (2010a) *La entrevista, una invención dialógica* [*The Interview: A Dialogic Invention*]. Buenos Aires: Paidós.

Arfuch, Leonor (2010b) *O Espaço Biográfico. Dilemas da Subjetividade Contemporânea* [*On Biographical Space: Dilemmas of Contemporary Subjectivity*], trans. Paloma Vidal. Rio de Janeiro: EDUERJ.

Arfuch, Leonor (2012) 'El presente del pasado. Ética y responsabilidad' ['The Present and the Past: Ethics and Responsibility'], in Anne Huffschmid and Valeria Durán (eds), *Topografías conflictivas* [*Conflicted Topographies*]. Buenos Aires: Trilce, pp. 31–43.

Arfuch, Leonor (2013) *Memoria y autobiografía: exploraciones en los límites* [*Memory and Autobiography: Explorations at the Limits*]. Buenos Aires: Fondo de Cultura Económica.

Aubrey, John (1987) *Aubrey's Brief Lives*. London: Penguin Classics.

Augé, Marc (2011) *La Vie en Double. Voyage, ethnologie, ecriture* [*Double Life: Journey, Ethnology, Writing*]. Paris: Payot et Rivage.

Authier, Jacqueline (1982) 'Hétérogénéité montrée et hétérogénéité constitutive: elements pour une approche de l'autre dans le discours' ['Shown and Constitutive Heterogeneity: Elements of an Approach, to the Other in Discourse'], in DRLAV, *Revue de Linguistique* 26: 91–151.

Bachelard, Gaston (1964) *The Poetics of Space*, trans. Maria Jolas. New York: Orion Press.

Bachmann, Ingeborg and Celan, Paul (2010) *Correspondence*, trans. Weilan Hoban. Kolkata, India: Seagull Books.

Bakhtin, Mikhail (1978) *Théorie et Esthétique du Roman*. Paris: Gallimard.

Bakhtin, Mikhail (1990) *Art and Answerability: Early Philosophical Essays*, ed. Caryl Emerson and Mikhail Bakhtin, trans. Michael Holquist. Austin: University of Texas Press.

Bakhtin, Mikhail (1992) *The Dialogic Imagination: Four Essays*. Austin: University of Texas Press.

Bakhtin, Mikhail (1993) *Toward a Philosophy of the Act*, trans. Vadin Liapunov. Austin: University of Texas Press.

Barthes, Roland (1977) *Roland Barthes by Roland Barthes*, trans. Richard Howard. New York: Farrar, Straus and Giroux.

Barthes, Roland (1979a) *A Lover's Discourse: Fragments*, trans. Richard Howard. London: Jonathan Cape.

Barthes, Roland (1979b) *The Eiffel Tower and Other Mythologies*, trans. Richard Howard. New York: Farrar, Straus and Giroux.

Barthes, Roland (1983) *Empire of Signs*, trans. Richard Howard. New York: Hill & Wang.

Barthes, Roland (1989) 'The Reality Effect', in *The Rustle of Language*, trans. Richard Howard. Berkeley: University of California Press, pp. 141–8.

Barthes, Roland (2005) *The Neutral: Lecture Course at the College de France (1977–1978)*, trans. Rosalind E. Krauss and Denis Hollier. New York: Columbia University Press.

Barthes, Roland (2010a) *The Preparation of the Novel: Lecture Courses and Seminars at the Collège de France (1978–1979 and 1979–1980)*, trans. Kate Briggs. New York: Columbia University Press.

Barthes, Roland (2010b) *Mourning Diary*, trans. Richard Howard. New York: Hill and Wang.

Barthes, Roland (2013) *How to Live Together: Novelistic Simulations of Some Everyday Spaces*, trans. Kate Briggs. New York: Columbia University Press.

Beguán, Viviana, Kozameh, Alicia and Echarte, Silvia (2006) *Nosotras, las presas políticas. 1974–1983* [*We, Political Prisoners: 1974–1983*]. Buenos Aires: Nuestra América.

Belzagui, Pablo René (2010 [2007]) *No matar. Sobre la responsa-bilidad* [*No Killing. On Responsibility*], vols 1 and 2. Cordoba: Del Cíclope/University of Cordoba.

Benjamin, Walter (1968) *Illuminations*, trans. Harry Zohn. New York: Harcourt, Brace & World.

Benjamin, Walter (1998) *The Origin of German Tragic Drama*, trans. John Osborne. London: Verso.

Benveniste, Émile (1973) *Problems in General Linguistics*, trans. Mary Elizabeth Meek. Miami: University of Miami Press.

Berlant, Lauren (1998) 'Intimacy: A Special Issue', *Critical Inquiry* 24(2): 281–8.

Bolaño, Roberto (2009) *Nazi Literature in the Americas*, trans. Chris Andrews. Cambridge, MA: New Directions.

Bolaño, Roberto (2008) *2666*, trans. Natasha Wimmer. New York: Farrar, Straus and Giroux.

Boltanski, Christian and Grenier, Catherine (2009) *The Possible Life of Christian Boltanski*, trans. Marc Lowenthal. Boston: Museum of Fine Arts.

Bonasso, Miguel (1984) *Recuerdo de la muerte* [*Remembrance of Death*]. Buenos Aires: Bruguera.

Bourdieu, Pierre (1998) *Practical Reason*. Cambridge: Polity Press.

Burucúa, Gastón (2007) 'Contar la masacre' ['Telling the Massacre'] (interview with Hugo Montero), *Nómada*, 6 August.

Butler, Judith (1998) *The Psychic Life of Power: Theories in Subjection*. Stanford, CA: Stanford University Press.

Butler, Judith (2004) *Precarious Life: The Powers of Mourning and Violence*. London: Verso.

Butler, Judith (2005) *Giving an Account of Oneself*. New York: Fordham University Press.

Calveiro, Pilar (2006) *Poder y desaparición. Los campos de concentración en la Argentina* [*Power and Disappearance: Concentration Camps in Argentina*]. Buenos Aires: Colihue.

Calveiro, Pilar (2012) *Violencias de Estado* [*State Violence*]. Buenos Aires: Siglo xxi.

Castellanos, Rosario (1998) *Obras II: Poesía, Teatro y Ensayo*. Mexico City: Fondo de Cultura Economica.

Cavarero, Adriana (2009) *Horrorism: Naming Contemporary Violence*, trans. William McCuaig. New York: Columbia University Press.

Ciollaro, Noemí (1999) *Pájaros sin luz. Testimonios de mujeres de desaparecidos* [*Birds without Light: Testimonies of Wives of the Disappeared*]. Buenos Aires: Planeta.

Cortázar, Julio (2009) *Papeles inesperados* [*Unexpected Papers*]. Barcelona: Alfaguara.

Davoine, Françoise and Gaudillière, Jean-Max (2004) *History Beyond Trauma*, trans. Susan Fairfield. New York: Other Press.

De Alba, Alicia (2007) *Curriculum-Society: The Weight of Uncertainty, the Strength of Imagination*. Mexico City: UNAM-IISUE.

De Certeau, Michel (1984) *The Practice of Everyday Life*, trans. Steven Rendall. Berkeley: University of California Press.

De Lauretis, Teresa (1984) *Alicia Doesn't: Feminism, Semiotics, Cinema*. Bloomington: Indiana University Press.

Del Barco, Oscar (2007) 'No matarás', *Journal of Latin American Cultural Studies* 16(2): 115–17.

De Man, Paul (1984) 'Autobiography as De-facement', in *The Rhetoric of Romanticism*. New York: Columbia University Press, pp. 67–81.

Deleuze, Gilles (2007) *Two Regimes of Madness: Texts and Interviews 1975–1995*, trans. Ames Hodges and Mike Taormina. Paris: Semiotext(e).

Derrida, Jacques (1982) 'Tympan', in *Margins of Philosophy*, trans. Alan Bass. Chicago: Chicago University Press.

Derrida, Jacques (2000) 'A Self-Unsealing Poetic Text', in Michael P. Clark (ed.), *Revenge of the Aesthetic: The Place of Literature in Theory Today*, trans. Rachel Bowlby. Berkeley/Los Angeles: University of California Press.

Deutsche, Rosalyn (2007) Seminar in the series *Ideas recibidas. Un vocabulario para la cultura artística contemporánea* [*Received Ideas: A Vocabulary for Contemporary Artistic Culture*] at Barcelona Museum of Contemporary Art (MACBA), 19 November.

Diana, Marta (1996) *Mujeres guerrilleras. Sus testimonios en la militancia de los setenta* [*Women Guerrilleras: Their Testimonies during the Militancy of the Seventies*]. Buenos Aires: Planeta.

Didi-Huberman, Georges (2008) *Images in Spite of All: Four Photographs from Auschwitz*, trans. Shane B. Lillis. Chicago: Chicago University Press.

Didi-Huberman, Georges, Pollock, Griselda and Rancière, Jacques (2007) *Alfredo Jaar. La politique des images* [*Alfredo Jaar: The Politics of Images*]. Zurich: JRP/Ringier.

Dosse, François (2007) *El arte de la biografía* [*The Art of Biography*]. Mexico City: Universidad Ibero-americana.

Dosse, François (2009) *Gilles Deleuze and Félix Guattari: Intersecting Lives*, trans. Deborah Glassman. New York: Columbia University Press.

Felski, Rita (1989) *Beyond Feminist Aesthetics: Feminist Literature and Social Change*. Cambridge, MA: Harvard University Press.

Fondebrider, Jorge (2012) 'Georges Perec: instrucciones para una vida de palabras' ['Georges Perec: Instructions for a Life of Words'], *Revista de Cultura Ñ*, Clarín. Buenos Aires, 24 August.

Friedländer, Saul (ed.) (1992) *Probing the Limits of Representation: Nazism and the 'Final Solution'*. London/Cambridge, MA: Harvard University Press.

Gadamer, Hans-Georg (1975) *Truth and Method*, trans. Joel

Weinsheimer and Donald G. Marshall. London/New York: Bloomsbury.

García Canclini, Néstor (2003) 'Malentendidos interculturales en la frontera México–Estados Unidos' ['Cultural Misunderstandings on the Mexico–United States Border'], in José Luis García and Ascensión Barañano (eds), *Culturas en contacto. Encuentros y desencuentros* [*Cultures in Contact: Meetings and Non-Meetings*]. Madrid: Ministerio de Educación, Cultura y Deporte de España.

Giddens, Anthony (1993) *The Transformation of Intimacy: Sexuality, Love and Eroticism in Modern Societies*. Cambridge: Polity.

Gilmore, Leigh (1994) *Autobiographics: A Feminist Theory of Women's Self-Representation*. Ithaca and London: Cornell University Press.

Gilmore, Leigh (2001) *The Limits of Autobiography: Trauma and Testimony*. Ithaca and London: Cornell University Press.

Ginzburg, J., Hardman, F. and Seligman-Silva, M. (eds) (2012) *Escritas da violência* [*Writings on Violence*], vol. 2. Rio de Janeiro: 7Letras.

Greimas, Algirdas J. (1987) *On Meaning: Selected Writing in Semiotic Theory*, trans. P. J. Perron and F. H. Collins. Minneapolis: University of Minnesota Press.

Grice, H. Paul (1975) 'Logic and Conversation', in Peter Cole and Jerry L. Morgan (eds), *Syntax and Semantics, Vol. 3: Speech Acts*. New York: Academic Press.

Guasch, Anna Maria (ed.) (2010) *La memoria del otro. Catálogo* [*Memory of the Other. Catalogue*]. Santiago, Chile: Museo Nacional de Bellas Artes.

Habermas, Jürgen (1989) *The Structural Transformation of the Public Sphere*, trans. Thomas Berger and Frederick Lawrence. Cambridge, MA: Massachusetts Institute of Technology.

Halbwachs, Maurice (1992) *On Collective Memory*, ed. and trans. Lewis A. Coser. Chicago/London: University of Chicago Press.

Hayner, Priscilla (2001) *Unspeakable Truths*. New York: Routledge.

Heidegger, Martin (1971) *Poetry, Language, Thought*, trans. Albert Hofstadter. New York: Harper and Row.

Heidegger, Martin (2001) 'Poetically Man Dwells', in *Poetry, Language, Thought*. New York: HarperCollins, p. 225.

Heidegger, Martin (2008) *Letters to His Wife 1915–1970*, trans. R. D. V. Glasgow. Cambridge: Polity.

Heker, Liliana (2012) *The End of the Story*, trans. Andrea Labinger. Winsor, Canada: Biblioasis.

Holroyd, Michael (1970) 'Out of Print', *The American Scholar* 39(2): 310–17.

Holroyd, Michael (1996) *Augustus John: The New Biography*. London: Chatto and Windus.

Holroyd, Michael (1999) *Basil Street Blues*. London: Little, Brown and Company.

Holroyd, Michael (2002) *Works on Paper: The Craft of Biography and Autobiography*. London: Little Brown.

Huffschmidt, A. and Durán, V. (eds) (2012) *Topografías conflictivas* [*Conflict Topographies*]. Buenos Aires: Trilce.

Jaar, Alfredo (2006) *Jaar SCL 2006*. Barcelona: Actar.

Laclau, Ernesto (2000) *Misticismo, retórica y política* [*Mysticism, Rhetoric and Politics*]. Buenos Aires: Fondo de Cultura Económica.

Laclau, Ernesto and Mouffe, Chantal (2001) *Hegemony and Social Strategy: Towards a Radical Democratic Politics*. London: Verso.

Lash, Scott (2007) 'Capitalism and Metaphysics', *Theory, Culture and Society* 24(5): 1–26.

Lejeune, Philippe (1975) *Le pacte autobiographique* [*The Autobiographical Pact*]. Paris, Seuil.

Levinas, Emmanuel (1985) *Ethics and Infinity*, trans. Richard A. Cohen. Pittsburgh: Duquesne University Press.

Levinas, Emmanuel (1987) *Time and the Other*, trans. Richard A. Cohen. Pittsburgh: Duquesne University Press.

Lipovetsky, Gilles and Serroy, Jean (2008) *La Culture-monde. Réponse a une société désorientée* [*The Culture-World: Response to a Disoriented Society*]. Paris: Odile Jacob.

Longoni, Ana (2007) *Traiciones* [*Betrayals*]. Buenos Aires: Norma.

Loraux, Nicole (2002) *The Divided City: On Memory and Forgetting in Ancient Athens*, trans. Corinne Pache and Jeff Fort. Cambridge, MA: MIT Press.

Ludmer, Josefina (2011) *Aquí América Latina. Una especulación* [*Here Latin America: A Speculation*]. Buenos Aires: Eterna Cadencia.

Massey, Doreen (2005) *For Space*. London: Sage.

Mitchell, W. J. T. (1996) 'What Do Pictures Really Want?' *October* 77: 71–82.

Molloy, Sylvia (1991) *At Face Value: Autobiographical Writing in Spanish America*. Cambridge, UK/New York: Cambridge University Press

Molloy, Sylvia and Siskind, Mariano (2006) *Poéticas de la distancia. Adentro y afuera de la literatura argentina* [*The Poetics of Distance: Inside and Outside Argentinian Literature*]. Buenos Aires: Norma.

Mouffe, Chantal (2005) *On the Political* (*Thinking in Action*). London/New York: Routledge.

Mouffe, Chantal (2007) 'Art and Democracy: Art as an Agonistic Intervention in Public Space', *Art As a Public Issue*, 1 January.

Nancy, Jean-Luc (2005) *The Ground of the Image*, trans. Jeff Fort. New York: Fordham University Press.

Orozco, Olga (1998) 'El Narrador', in *En el revés del cielo*. Cordoba, Argentina: Alción Editora.

Perec, Georges (1990) *Je Suis Né [I Am Born]*. Paris: Éditions du Seuil.

Propp, Vladimir (1968) *Morphology of the Folktale*, trans. Laurence Scott. Austin: University of Texas Press.

Rancière, Jacques (1999) *Dis-agreement: Politics and Philosophy*, trans. Julie Rose. Minneapolis/London: University of Minnesota Press.

Reguillo, Rossana (2012) 'The Narco-Machine and the Work of Violence: Notes towards Its Decodification', trans. Margot Olavarría, *Hemispheric* 8(2). Available at: http://hemi.nyu.edu/hemi/en/e-misferica-82/reguillo.

Reyes, Alfonso (1984) *Retratos reales e imaginarios [Real and Imagined Portraits]*. Barcelona: Bruguera.

Richard, Nelly (2010) *Crítica de la memoria [A Critique of Memory]*. Santiago de Chile: Universidad Diego Portales.

Ricoeur, Paul (1984/1985/1988) *Time and Narrative*, 3 vols, trans. Kathleen McLaughlin, Kathleen Blamey and David Pellauer. Chicago: University of Chicago Press.

Ricoeur, Paul (1992) *Oneself as Other*, trans. Kathleen McLaughlin, Kathleen Blamey and David Pellauer. Chicago: University of Chicago Press.

Ricoeur, Paul (2004) *Memory, History, Forgetting*, trans. Kathleen McLaughlin, Kathleen Blamey and David Pellauer. Chicago: University of Chicago Press.

Robin, Régine (1996) *Identidad, memoria, relato. La imposible narración de sí mismo [Identity, Memory, Story: An Impossible Narrative]*. Buenos Aires: Serie Cuadernos de Posgrado, Facultad de Ciencias Sociales/cbc.

Robin, Régine (2009) *Mégapolis. Les derniers pas du flâneur [Megapolis: The Past Steps of of the Flaneur]*. Paris: Stock.

Romano Sued, Susana (2007) *Procedimiento. Memoria de La Perla y La Rivera [Procedures: Memory of La Perla and La Rivera]*. Córdoba: El Emporio.

Saer, Juan José (2012) *Papeles de trabajo [Working Papers]*. Buenos Aires: Seix Barral.

Salvi, Valentina (2012) 'Sobre memorias parciales y memoria completa. Prácticas conmemorativas y narrativa cívico-militar sobre el pasado reciente en Argentina' ['On Partial Memories and Complete Memories: Commemorative Practices and Civic-Military Narrative on the Recent Past in Argentina'], in Anne Huffschmid and Valeria Durán (eds), *Topografías conflictivas* [*Conflictive Topographies*]. Buenos Aires: Trilce, pp. 265–81.

Sarlo, Beatriz (2005) *Tiempo pasado. Cultura de la memoria y giro subjetivo. Una Discusión.* [*Time Past: The Culture of Memory and the Subjective Turn: A Discussion*]. Buenos Aires: Siglo xxi.

Schweizer, Nicole (2007) 'The Politics of Images: An Introduction', in Georges Didi-Huberman et al. (eds), *Alfredo Jaar. La politique des images* [*Alfredo Jaar: The Politics of Images*]. Zurich: JRP/Ringier.

Schwob, Marcel (1924) *Imaginary Lives*. New York: Boni and Liveright.

Scott, Joan (1991) 'The Evidence of Experience', *Critical Inquiry* 17(4): 773–97.

Sebald, W. G. (1998) *The Rings of Saturn*, trans. Michael Hulse. London: Harvill Press.

Sebald, W. G. (2001) *Austerlitz*, trans. Anthea Bell. New York: Random House.

Sebald, W. G. (2004) *On the Natural History of Destruction*, trans. Anthea Bell. London: Penguin.

Sennett, Richard (1990) *The Conscience of the Eye: The Design and Social Life of Cities*. New York/London: Norton.

Simmel, Georg (2002) *Cuestiones fundamentales de sociología*. Barcelona: Gedisa.

Smith, Neil (1996) *The New Urban Frontier: Gentrification and the Revanchist City*. London/New York: Routledge.

Smith, Sidonie (2002) *Interfaces: Women, Autobiography, Image, Performance*. Ann Arbor: University of Michigan Press.

Sontag, Susan (2003) *Regarding the Pain of Others*. London: Picador.

Stegmayer, María (2012) 'Zonas de inquietud' ['Zones of Disquiet'], in 'Zonas de inquietud. Poder, violencia y memoria en la literatura argentina (1995–2010)' ['Zones of Disquiet: Power, Violence and Memory in Argentinian Literature']. Unpublished PhD thesis. Facultad de Ciencias Sociales, Universidad de Buenos Aires, p. 56.

Tatián, Diego (2007) 'Letter from Diego Tatián', *Journal of Latin American Cultural Studies* 16(2): 141–3.

Todorov, Tzvetan (1984) *Mikhail Bakhtin: The Dialogic Principle*, trans. Wlad Godzich. Manchester and New York: Manchester University Press.

Todorov, Tzvetan (2000). *Les abus de la mémoire* [*The Abuses of Memory*]. Paris: Arléa.

Todorov, Tzvetan (2008) *Duties and Delights: The Life of a Go-Between*. Chicago: University of Chicago Press.

Tozzi, V. and Lavagnino, N. (eds) (2012) *Hayden White. La escritura del pasado y el futuro de la historiografía* [*Hayden White: The Writing of the Past and the Future of Historiography*]. Buenos Aires: EDUNTREF.

Vattimo, Gianni (2010) *Not Being God: A Collected Autobiography*, trans. William McCuaig. New York: Columbia University Press.

Vezzetti, Hugo (2009) *Sobre la violencia revolucionaria* [*On Revolutionary Violence*]. Buenos Aires: Siglo xxi.

White, Hayden (1987) *The Content of Form: Narrative Discourse and Historical Representation*. Baltimore: The Johns Hopkins University Press.

White, Hayden (2005) 'Historical Fiction, Fictional History and Historical Reality', *Rethinking History* 9: 147–57.

Williams, Raymond (1985) *Keywords: The Vocabulary of Culture and Society*. New York: Oxford University Press.

Wittgenstein, Ludwig (1953) *Philosophical Investigations*, trans. G. E. M. Anscombe, P. M. S. Hacker and Joachim Schulte. London: Basil Blackwell.

Woolf, Virginia (1974) 'The Art of Biography', in *The Death of the Moth and Other Essays*. San Diego, CA: Harcourt Brace Jovanovich.

Yerushalmi, Yosef, Loraux, Nicole, Mammsen, Hans, Milner, Jean-Claude and Vattino, Gianni (1989) *Usos del olvido* [*Uses of Forgetting*]. Buenos Aires: Nueva Visión.

Young, James E. (2000) *At Memory's Edge*. New Haven and London: Yale University Press.

References to films

A Letter from Greenpoint (2004), dir. Jonas Mekas.

Patience (after Sebald) (2012), dir. Grant Gee.

Jeanne Dielman, 23 quai du Commerce, 1080 Bruxelles (1975), dir. Chantal Akerman.

De l'autre côté (2002), dir. Chantal Akerman.

JLG/JLG (1995), dir. Jean-Luc Godard.

References to visual artworks

Christian Boltanski:
Search for and Presentation of Everything Remaining from My Childhood 1944–50 (1969).

Attempt at Reconstitution of Objects that Belonged to Christian Boltanski between 1948 and 1954 (1970–71).
10 Portrait Photographs of Christian Boltanski 1946–1964 (1972).
Les Saynètes Comiques [One-Act Comedies] (1974).
Photo Album of the Family D., 1939–1964 (1975).
Storage Area of the Children's Museum, Musée d'art Moderne de la Ville de Paris (1989).
6 Septembres [*September 6th*] (2005).
Personne in Monumenta (2010).

Nury González:
Sueño velado [*Waking Dream*] (2009).
Sobre la historia natural de la destrucción [*On the Natural History of Destruction*] (2011).

Antoni Muntadas:
On Translation/Fear/Miedo (2005).
On Translation/Miedo/Jauf (2007).

Krzysztof Wodiczko:
The Hiroshima Projection (1999).
The Tijuana Projection (2002).

Francis Alÿs, http://www.francisalys.com/:
The Loop (1997).
The Green Line (2005).

Alfredo Jaar, http://www.alfredojaar.net/index1.html:
From *The Rwanda Project*:
Signs of Life (1994).
Untitled (*Newsweek*) (1994).
Real Pictures (1995).
The Eyes of Gutete Emerita (1996).
The Silence of Nduwayezu (1997).
From *Art on the Frontier*:
La Nube/The Cloud (2000).

Geometría de la Conciencia [*The Geometry of the Conscience*], permanent exhibit in the Museo de la Memoria y los Derechos Humanos, Santiago de Chile.

Index

Kindertransport xvi, 129n 4
Kingsmill, Hugh 126n 61
Kirchner, Nestor 131n 8
Kruger, Barbara 101
Kwak Bok Soon 111, 112

La Intemperie magazine 77,
 109
*La Memoria del Otro (The
 Memory of the Other)*
 video art exhibition 94
Lacan, Jacques 49, 56
Laclau, Ernesto xiv
 *Mysticism, Rhetoric and
 Politics* 85
language xxii, 48
 configurative role of 50–1
 pictorial capacity 41
 retrospective speech 25–6
 and transgression 89–94
 see also narration;
  testimony
Larkin, Philip 125n 58
Lash, Scott 91
Leiris, Michel 1
Lejeune, Philippe xii, xiv
Lenin, Vladimir 80
Levi, Primo 59
Levinas, Emmanuel 17, 87–8,
 98, 110, 129n 12
Lewin, Miriam xxii, 58
limit 89, 92, 116
 see also frontier zones
listening
 act of hearing 1, 3
 and the construction of the
  subject 64–5
 corporal listening 51
'lives and letters' conception of
 biography 27–8
Loraux, Nicole xix, 129n 9
Los Angeles 10
Los rubios (film) 132n 12
Ludmer, Josefina ix, 93

M (film) 132n 12
manuscripts, recovering 125n
 58
Mao Zedong 80
marginality 1
market logics, impersonalizing
 dynamics of xii
Massey, Doreen xiv, 9, 91
media confessional 4
media memory 44
media sensationalism 3
Mekas, Jonas, *A Letter from
 Greenpoint* 121n 7
memoirs 3
*Memoirs of Camps.
 Photographs of Nazi
 Concentration Camps*
 (exhibition) 128n 90
memorials and monuments 6,
 44, 53, 116
memory
 abuses of 6
 biographical memory 12
 collective memory xix, 12,
  41, 43, 44, 54
 counter-memories 53–4
 as dilemma 54
 ethical obligation of 53
 historical memory 12
 lost memories, search for 45
 memorial inflation 6
 politics of 6, 53, 69, 84
 temporalities of 6, 12, 45,
  48, 58, 61, 84, 137n 58
 transmission of 40, 43, 44,
  45
 urban markers 12
memory value 5, 7
metaphor 69
 see also traumatic memory
metonymy 69
Mew, Charlotte 126n 61
Mexico City 10
migrants 7, 91, 95